Introduction

The book of Jeremiah chapter 1 verses 4-5 in the New King James Version says,

4 Then the word of the Lord came unto me, saying,

5 Before I formed thee in the belly I knew thee; and before thou camest forth out of the womb I sanctified thee, and I ordained thee a prophet unto the nations.

Fear not brothers and sisters just as God knew Jeremiah before he was formed in the belly of his mother he also knows us. God has predestined our paths for the bible tells us, "In whom also we have obtained an in heritance, being predestined according to the purpose of him who worketh all things after the counsel of his own will" (Ephesians 1:11). Beloved we are predestined for greatness!

I will attempt to show you in this book that I have written that although we go through many trials and tribulations in our life and sometimes it seems as though you want to throw in the towel DON"T! Although it seems that you don't want to live this life any longer because you've experienced so much heartache and pain DON'T GIVE UP!

We may not understand the plans that God has for our lives but believe me when I tell you there is a plan. Part of the plan is to see us living in our God given potential. Everyone has the potential to be great in any aspect of their lives. We just have to tap in to what it is and the only way to do that is tap into the presence of God.

So brothers and sisters I have written this book in hopes that it will encourage someone to not give up the fight. If you believe in God then you must believe there is a devil. I once heard someone say, "The devils greatest deception to mankind is making them believe that he does not exist". He doesn't want us to be great, he doesn't want us to live, he wants us to hate ourselves and hate others which can only cause destruction not only to ourselves but to others as well. Believe it or not he wants us dead.

But here is the good news... Psalm 34:8 tells us, "O taste and see that the Lord is good; blessed is the man who trusts in Him!" We can live life, obtain happiness, live in our potential and be great on this earth if we trust and believe that God will reward those who seek him!

I hope and pray that you will be blessed when you read this book. As for me the devil thought he had me but because God loves me so much and loves you so much we will not be defeated. We will live and not die!

The Bible says, "For God so loved the world, that he gave his only begotten Son, that whosoever believeth in him should not perish, but have everlasting life" (St. John 3:16). Let us choose life today!

Be Blessed,

Evangelist Tyraine

I

I was born in Brooklyn New York, the first of four children. My mother is a West Indian Cuban and my father is a Japanese Negro. The combination of cultures caused me to be a very beautiful baby and that's one of the reasons why she never understood why her father didn't want me. When I was 2 years old my father dangled me over the Staten Island Ferry. My father was a heroin addict, a junkie, and maybe he did it because if he had gotten rid of me there would be more money to get drugs and get high or maybe he didn't know what he was doing. My mother told me that while he was holding me on the ferry she turned around for a moment, and when she turned back around to get me he was holding my feet and was dangling me over the railing of the boat. She screamed, begged and cried for him not to drop me but, she said he just laughed and laughed. Minutes later he bought my little body back overboard laughing hysterically. That was my first brush with death at the age of 2, what a way to start life.

I remember my mother and father fighting one day. The reason for the fight was because he stole our Easter clothes to buy heroin. My mother was in the kitchen ironing clothes when the fight started. As they started to argue she lifted the iron in the air as if she was getting ready to bust his head wide open with it and my junkie father stood across from her with a knife ready to protect himself by any means necessary. In that kitchen there was loud arguing, yelling, they were calling each other names that I do not want to repeat. Suddenly, there was a knock at the door. It was the police! Thank

God someone called the cops. But they weren't there because of the fight though; they were there to arrest my father. There was a robbery a couple of days prior to the argument with my mother. Someone robbed the subway token booth clerk and gave a description of the thief. The description lined up with my father's description and he had previous warrants and arrests so I wasn't difficult to get an address on him. The police took him away in handcuffs. Bye, Bye... that would be the last time I saw my father.

My mother is very beautiful. Up until this day her skin is flawless, she still has all of her teeth and can think very clearly. So of course shortly after my father was taken away she began dating again. We lived in Brooklyn at the time, in a one bedroom apartment. My brother, my sister and I slept in the living room on a sofa bed and my mother slept in the bedroom. In those days it wasn't about the comfort of the children but the comfort of the one who was paying the bills and buying the food. Some of the kids these days have it all backward, they think that the world revolves around but it doesn't. My mother soon met a man and was dating. She deserved some fun and happiness after all that my father the junkie put her through. One night my mother decided that it was time we met the man that she was going out with. I guess she really liked him and wanted us to meet him. I was about 7 years old at the time and excited for my mother. When he came to the house and we were introduced to him, something inside of me did not feel comfortable I guess it a child's intuition. I've heard people say that a child spirit is innocent and when evil comes around they can feel it so when he looked at me I got a very uncomfortable, uneasy feeling about him. After that incident, he came around quite frequently, hell, after a while he moved in with us, in that little ole one bedroom apartment and slept in the room with my mom. After he was around for a while my mother wanted to change his status to our father, she wanted us to begin to call him daddy. One day, as we were all seated around the dinner table, my mother spoke to us individually and told us that for now on we were to call him Daddy. My siblings did what they were told but I wasn't going to call him Daddy. My mother and her new boyfriend turned looked at me, my mother opened her mouth and said to me, "I want you to start getting used to calling him Daddy. Can you do that? Let me hear you say Daddy". I gave her a blank stare. "Say Daddy now" my mother told me. I looked at both of them and said, "I'll never call him Daddy, he's not my father and never will be. I will call him by his name and that's what I'm going to call him". He and my mother looked at each other shocked and in awe because I told them what I was going to do and not what they wanted me to do. So for the rest of his life I called him by his first name. Until the day he died I called him by his first name.

The devil's job is to steal, kill and destroy our lives from the time we are born until the time that we die. He cunning, tricky and will use the subtlest of situations to mess with your mind and your body to destroy you. In my case, he used my mother's boyfriend when I was just 7 years old.

My mother promised to raise me as in the Catholic faith. According to the Catholic religion, the first born of every family, whether it is a son or daughter, must be dedicated back to the Catholic Church. My mother was raised Catholic because my Grandfather was a Roman

Catholic. He dedicated her back and she was his first born, so being that I was her first born she had to do the same. I made my first communion in the church, I attended religious studies, I was baptized in St. Paul's Catholic Church and my first confession was in the church by the age of 7. That's when the devil that it was time to mess with me again.

I did not care for that man. He often made me feel creepy inside. I learned to tolerate him for my mother's sake. My mother went to school during the days and she often worked at night. One of my Aunt's would babysit us while she was out. One night my Aunt had and emergency and could not babysit us as she normally did so he had to do it. It was late at night and my mother did not get home from work yet. He asked me if I knew how to make coffee that night. What little girl would not want to make coffee for the man of the house? So I told him that I did. Then he asked," How do you make a pot of coffee little girl?" so I told him how I would make the coffee. Innocently I explained how I would put the coffee grounds inside of the filter, measure out the water, put it into the machine and turn it on and he just started to laugh. I guess because he was laughing I started to laugh too not realizing that he was luring me into a trap. The couch in the living room was already pulled out into a bed, my sister and brother were in the only bedroom watching television, and it was the perfect opportunity for him to attack. He picked me up and put me on the bed, he was tickling me so hard that I was frantic with laughter. Laughing the way a daughter would when being tickled by her father. Then he attacked. He pulled the blanket over us still tickling me, and then he went to the place that was forbidden to men. He slid my little panties to the side, working his fingers near my most private parts and I felt a sensation that I had never experienced before. This act of touching, feeling, penetrating a place that is supposed to be forbidden to men went on for a couple of minutes and then it stopped. Although that process had stopped, the scaring process had begun...

After that incident, I felt that maybe I had did something wrong but I wasn't sure. My mother and her boyfriend would be in the bed watching television or talking and they seemed to be so happy. I was happy because she was happy but I couldn't understand why I was not included in their fun. Oh well, maybe something was wrong with what had happened so I began to block the memory of that night into a compartment in my brain hoping that it would never resurface again. We lived in

the Bronx then.

About a year later we moved back to Brooklyn

from the Bronx. I liked Brooklyn because I was born there

in Kings County Hospital. As a matter of fact in Brooklyn

was the first time I encountered this man. We moved

into a two family house in the Bushwick section of

Brooklyn. There were nice houses on the street where we

lived, and the elementary school was two blocks away so I

could walk to school every day with my friends. I was so

excited to meet new friends, new teachers and have fun

all day in school. I loved school. I was a very bright,

intelligent and my future was promising. I was so gifted

that one evening my 3rd grade teacher and his wife visited

our home to speak to my mother about me. They told

her that I was an exceptionally bright child and wanted

me to be in the honors classes because I had a brilliant mind. My mother was so proud of me and I was so proud of myself that every day thereafter I went to school with my head held high. My head was raised as high as the clouds in the sky because I considered myself to be smarter and brighter than the rest of the kids in my class. Shoot, smarter and brighter than the kids in the whole school.

It was quite ironic, that the people who lived downstairs had the same last name that we did but there was something weird about them. They were sisters, probably in their 40's and unmarried. We seldom saw them but, sometimes a smell would come up into our house from theirs. It did not smell like someone was cooking food, it smelled like someone was burning candles or incense. Besides the stink odor there were sounds occasionally, they sounded like chanting or singing. One night my mother was reading the book the "Exorcist", why she was reading it I don't know but, as I was in my bed sleeping, she started screaming. It was a high pitched deafening scream that made me jump out of my bed and into her room which was right next to mine. I jumped on top of her bed to hold her when she told me that while she was reading the book her bed began to shake. At the time I wasn't sure if I believed it or not. I didn't feel it myself but I believed her, after all she is my mother. In any event I always thought there was something evil about that house.

One day after school, when I got home I was so hungry I could've eaten a horse but, being that I did not live on a farm and there weren't any horses I decided to look for something to eat in the cabinets and the refrigerator. When I opened the cabinets I saw what looked like little jars of things I've never seen or heard of. There were all sorts of herbs, roots and liquids. Something else was different in the house too. Every now and then music would be played that I never heard before. Some of it sounded like rivers or oceans, and some of it sounded like people chanting. Oh my God, it seemed to me that the people downstairs were rubbing off on him. It couldn't be my mother messing around with this stuff. Maybe he was putting spells on us while we were sleeping, maybe that's why my mother's bed was shaking or maybe it was just my imagination. Ma's boyfriend slept during the day because he worked at night therefore we had to be exceptionally quiet until he woke up at 5pm. One day I came home from school and he was already up. I was always the first one home so I was nervous because I was by myself. He called my name, I did not want to see what he wanted because I was afraid, but I went into their bedroom to see why he was calling me. I should've kept quiet and hid in the house until someone came home but I didn't. As I was walking towards the bedroom I was getting a weird feeling deep in my belly, the feeling that something was getting ready to go wrong. He was standing up, 6 feet tall and over 200 pounds, my nerves were twisting and turning in my stomach, I felt like I wanted to vomit. He told me to stand directly in front of him he had something to tell me. I did what I was told scared to death. He put his hand on my little nipples and said," I see you are getting older now and your little nipples are starting to protrude through your blouse" then he started to pinch them. "Ok you can go now" he said. In an instant I felt so dirty, he made me feel so dirty, I was so ashamed, what did I do to get treated in such a way? God help me! With tears in my eyes I wanted to just die! I was so hurt, humiliated, violated by this man. No child should have to live like this. Who can I tell? There's no one to tell. If I tell my mother would she believe me? Maybe if I tell her she will get rid of him. She won't believe me! He helps her pay the rent, buy food, no she will not get rid of him. They go to the movies, parties, they sleep together, and no she will not believe me I kept telling myself. I will have to just keep this to myself. If I do then there will be no arguing or fighting like she did with my father, there will be peace. Yes, I will keep this to myself so my mother can be happy, so there can be peace. Daddy where are you? Daddy why did you leave me? And then I remembered my biological father was in jail.

He never touched me physically again, he used another tactic to try and destroy me, he infiltrated my mind. You can do just about anything to a person physically but, when you begin to attack their mind, their psyche, it can control a person's physical being as well. Your mind is the control center of all thinking patterns so he began to instill fear into me, attack my mind with saying nasty things to me when my mother or family was not listening. He would look at me certain ways when my mother was not aware or, when the opportunity arose he would look at me and laugh. He would make me feel ashamed of who I was, he made me feel dirty. I began to stay away from home as much as I could, getting involved in after school activities or, I would stay at a friend's house longer than usual. I was even making sure that my brother and sister where home before I got there. I never wanted to be alone with him in the house ever again!

I became interested in the acting. I had been in many school plays and, plays outside of school. I wanted to be an actress. I was used to wearing a mask every day because of what was going on with that man in my house so I figured that acting is the career I'd pursue. I spent my JHS years involved in my academics, with my friends or taking acting lessons in downtown Brooklyn at the Henry Street Settlement. When it was time to get ready for High School I auditioned for 2 of the top schools for the arts in New York City. One was the High School for Performing Arts and the other was Erasmus Hall. I did not pass the audition for Performing Arts because I didn't cry on cue when I was performing my monologue from "A Raisin in the Sun" but I did pass my audition for Erasmus Hall using the same monologue. I didn't go to Erasmus although I would have liked to. At that time, in that part of Brooklyn, there were rapes being reported constantly, robberies taking place and my mother was against me going there. Instead I attended Edward R. Murrow High School. It was a newly built school on avenue M in Brooklyn specializing in journalism. When I finally received my schedule for school I was happy. My classes consisted of basic academics like English, World History and Algebra but, I also had classes such as Acting 101 and Closed Circuit Television so it wasn't so bad. It would be great! I can travel by myself in the mornings to school and come home all by myself in the evenings. Before school started my mother and I went to the school on Avenue M so that I knew how to get there alone. I was glad that I would be back home after school later than my sister and brother, that would mean that I'd spent less time in that monsters prescence.

One weekend, when I was 14 years old something happened. My siblings and I were playing in the house and we smelled smoke. We thought it was coming from the evil sisters who lived downstairs that burnt God knows what downstairs but it wasn't. It wasn't the usual smell of candles or incense, this time it smelled like rubber. As I was walking towards the direction of the smell I saw smoke coming out of the wall in the living room. I screamed that the smoke was coming through the wall and my step father grabbed us together, ran with us downstairs, out the front entrance and into the middle of the street. Apparently our neighbors, not the ones that lived downstairs were in the middle of the street as well. We were all standing outside waiting for the fire trucks to arrive. While we were waiting, other people began to come out of their houses into the street trying to find out what was going on. As the fire trucks were speeding down the street to put out the fire, I saw my mother. She was walking swiftly down the block searching the people's faces trying to find us. When she finally found us and hugged us she asked what was going on. Someone told her that there was a fire in one of the houses. She asked," Which house"? Yours they told her. When she heard that the fire was in our house, I saw disbelief and frantic in her eyes. She kept saying over and over again, "The rent money is in the Bible. The rent money is in the Bible" then she turned to me and began to hug me tightly. After the firemen finished putting out the fire, my mother asked them if it was ok to go into the house. They said it would be ok but be very careful. My mother and I went into the house, it was devastated. It was dark and wet, there was broken furniture everywhere. Did they really have to do all of that? My mother and I searched everywhere for that Bible, after all that's where the money was. After a couple of minutes we found it, thank God! My mother grabbed that book, opened it up and began to flip through the pages. Nothing! She turned that Bible upside down and inside out and still there was no money. Finally with tears in her eyes she said, "They didn't have to do that. Bad enough they destroyed the place but they didn't have to take our money too".

We had no money, no food and, no clothes to wear. We had to go to the nearest Social Services agency, better known as the Welfare Office and ask them to help us. That day, with just the clothes on our backs we had to sit in a cold, dirty, crowed, smelly office with no food to eat. It was taking a long time before the welfare worker called my mother in to speak to her so my mother came up with a plan. My mother told us that on the count of three, we all have to fall out on the floor, start screaming and acting bad so that they would want to get us out of the office. So she began to count, one...two...three, and when we heard the number three we did as we were told. We made so much noise that the workers came out of their little cubicles. Next thing I know, someone was calling my mother in to speak to her. That was fun! She knew what she was doing and her plan worked like a charm. Now someone will help us.

Fourteen is a special age. It is the age when a child really begins to feel like a teenager. For some strange reason when a child turns fourteen they feel like they've finally arrived to young adulthood. Maybe the reason could be that they can finally get their working paper and don't have to depend on their parents financially for everything. What a relief knowing that you can get a job, make your own money and do whatever you wanted to. But that was wishful thinking for me.

How can I work when I don't have a place to live? How

could I work when every other day we are in some

welfare hotel, homeless shelter, or in some social services

office begging for help? After living in a hotel for a

couple of weeks in New York City, we moved into a

housing shelter in the Brownsville section of Brooklyn.

The shelter was so much better than living in that sleazy

hotel. It was almost like we had our own apartment.

There were two bedrooms, a kitchen, bathroom and a

living room. All of the furniture was a light brown color

and made of wood. In one bedroom there was a full size

bed and a dresser and in the other room were two sets of

bunk beds made out of that same cheap looking wood as

the rest of the furniture in the house. The place wasn't

luxurious but at least we were all together, we were

warm and we didn't have to eat restaurant food. My

mother could cook some home cooked meals and we can sit at the table and eat together like we used to.

It was summertime and that was good because that meant that we could play outside longer. I missed my friends. It hurts your soul when you have developed relationships and for reasons beyond your control you lose them. So I would have to make new friends. That's it! I would go outside and find new people to make friends with. The shelter was located in a neighborhood that wasn't the best but, I would have to make the best of it. The apartment like quarters that we were in was part of a complex of apartments. Just like my family, everyone who lived there had similar problems. Either their home was burned down or they were evicted from where they had previously lived. In a way it felt like we were living in a fancy homeless shelter for people waiting for permanent housing. Many of the children there had behavioral issues, in other words they were bad. They probably had some psychological damaging just like me, which was a good thing because we could bond. My mother warned me to stay away from those children around the shelter; she wanted me to play with my brother and sister and no one else. Who is she to tell me who I can or can't play with? Where was she when he was playing with me? So I found a group of kids that saw hanging out in the front of the building which looked like they didn't have a care in the world. That was exactly what I needed, not to have a care in the world. One day I introduced myself to these so called forbidden children and began to just hang out around them. They didn't shoo me away so I figured it was cool. They made me feel as if I belonged and I did. In a way we were the same, we were homeless, we were teenagers and we all wanted to escape life.

I drank my first beer that summer at the age of 14. I didn't really like the taste of it but, they were all doing it so I figured that there was nothing really bad about it. One day when my mother was at work I went outside to hang out with my new friends. The man inside of my house was quite oblivious to what I was doing because he worked the night before and needed to sleep. Besides, it was summertime. In those days it was not that difficult to buy beer or cigarettes, all you would have to do is act like you were buying it for your mother or father. Usually the person who owned the store would ask you for a note from your parent and if you could provide the note they gave you what you wanted. So that's what we did, we gave the store owner a note saying that one of our parents wanted a bottle of beer and some cigarettes. Touchdown! We scored! We were able to buy a 40oz. bottle of Old English Malt Liquor and a pack of Kool cigarettes. On our way home we decided to go up unto the roof of one of the buildings to drink and smoke no one could see us there. My adrenaline was raising a mile a minute. You know that feeling you get in the pit of your stomach when you know that you are doing something wrong. This was the first time I would be drinking beer but deep down inside of me I felt as though I shouldn't be doing it. I had smoked a cigarette before when I was 12 years old but, couldn't afford the habit so I stopped. The day was hot, especially on top of the roof. One of my friends opened the bottle of beer took a swig and passed it to the next person. When it was my turn I invited the cold beer to my mouth as though it was an ice cold soda. We all drank out of the bottle, that's the way it's done in the hood, we had to pass it around to each other and chug alug chug alug! Between the three of us, we drank that whole bottle of Old English in 15 minutes flat.

I was drunk! I stumbled down the stairs from the roof to my house after we drank the whole bottle of beer. Luckily I didn't fall on the steps and bust my head. My head was hurting so bad. It was spinning around and around, spinning and spinning. Oh my God, what did I do, what was I thinking? I made my way to our little makeshift apartment, put my key into the door then headed directly to the bathroom. Thank God no one was in there. He was sleeping in the bedroom with the door closed so I was able to go in the bathroom and vomit my brains out. The way I was feeling was absolutely horrible! My head was spinning, the toilet was messed up and, my breath was horrific. I swore on everything I owned, which was nothing at the time, that I would never drink again!

But that was just a drunken promise because when you

get high and throw up it just makes it easier for you to do

it again. A few weeks had passed, the summer was

getting ready to end and, we were still in the shelter. One

day when my mother came home from work she received

a letter in the mail saying that there was an apartment

available in Astoria, Queens. Queens? Where the heck is

Queens? I've never heard of a place named Queens. It

was a three bedroom apartment available for occupancy

in September. At the sound of that news, we all jumped

for joy. No more living in the shelter. Let's see, I could

have my own room, my sister and brother could share a

room. No wait...They would give the room to my brother,

being that he is a boy and my sister and I would share a

room. No...I don't like that idea. Finally it was decided,

my brother would have the room and my sister and I

would share the other. In any event, we were all so happy that we were moving to this place called Queens it didn't make a difference who had what room.

In the middle of August wen traveled to Queens to see the new apartment. It was nice, I liked it! It was located in Astoria Queens, way down near the East River. When we'd gotten off the bus in Astoria Projects and I looked around, the scenery was completely different than what I was used to seeing. I was used to living in Brooklyn in tenement buildings, houses that weren't so high off of the ground. I was in awe of the multi-story buildings. We walked down to the building that we would be living in after we got off the bus. The building was facing the East River and, the only thing that was separating our building from the vast body of water was a gate that went all the way down along the borders for at least a mile. As we approached the building with the river in front of us there was a wonderful view of New York City. WOW! We could see the Empire State Building standing right in front of our building. We could sit outside of our building and look at the city. I guess this is better than Brooklyn. We entered the building and we were taken to the apartment that would be ours. As we walked through the front door, on the right was the living room, as we walked straight there was a kitchen and as we walked a couple of more steps on the right was the bathroom. After the bathroom there were two medium sized bedrooms and way in back of the apartment was a little small bedroom. Finally a place we could call home. The view was absolutely amazing too. I walked into the bedroom in the back of the house and looked out of the window. There was a park with swings, sliding board, handball court and some kids smoking weed. Kids smoking weed? I guess I'm really going to like this place after all.

       Well my mother accepted the apartment. We moved into the projects on the 1st of September that year. My mother chose to move in on the 1st so that she could situate us in schools before the starting day. My brother and sister were younger than I, they were still in J.H.S. so it really didn't make much of a difference to them what school they would be going to but it did for me. I would be a sophomore in Murrow High School in Brooklyn. But, how was I going to get to school every day? My mother gave me a choice, she said either I could travel back and forth to Brooklyn to go to school or I could go to the high school in the neighborhood. I chose to travel the 2 ½ hours back and forth to school every day.

Where am I? Oh my God! Am I in a hospital?
What happened to me? The last thing I remember is
being in an ambulance rushed to the hospital. Oh God! I
must be in the hospital. What happened to me? "It's too
early to tell if she's going to make it or not" I heard one of
the doctor's say. "An artery burst on the right side of her
brain causing profuse bleeding in her brain. The surgery
was a success. If she hadn't received the surgery when
she did she would have died. She's really lucky". I
wanted to ask the doctor so many questions, but every
time I would try to speak the words would not come out
of my mouth. I've heard people say who have been in a
coma that although they could not speak they could hear;
their sense of hearing became keener. I was in a coma
but I heard everything that was being said around me. I
heard the doctors when they came into my room to check

on me, I could hear when my family members were talking and I heard them when they cried. I heard when the priest came into my room and prayed over me and when the Rabbi came in a said blessings over me. All I could do was lay there.

This unfamiliarity, this darkness lasted for what seemed to be an eternity. When all you see is darkness and hear voices you have no perception of time. It had been one month that I've been lying in that hospital bed with people hoping and praying that I would come back to them. It had been one month that I could not speak, move or eat. Some people also say that if you keep talking to a person who is in a coma, hopefully they will wake up. One day my Aunt came to visit me in the hospital, she was the Aunt who prayed for me throughout my drug addiction but, I will get back to that. At the time I was in the hospital, I knew that she rarely came out of her house because she has a condition called Vertigo and it is difficult to travel like she used to. In any event, when she came to see me she told me that God told her to come out of her house, go to the hospital and pray for me. She came to the hospital and sat beside me and began praying for me. She prayed that God would grant me favor and spare my life; she prayed that God's perfect will be done in my life also. She kept saying that God has a plan for my life and I will live and not die. After she finished praying for me she asked me if I wanted some chocolate chip cookies or lemon coconut cake. I liked chocolate chip cookies but, lemon coconut cake was my favorite. Inside of my head my mouth was watering for a slice the cake. I could just taste the coconut. But, why is she asking me this, she knows that I can't eat anything, can't she see the feeding tubes, maybe she's going to ask the nurses to feed it to me intravenously or through the tube. Of course I could not answer her, "why is she torturing me?" I'm asking myself. Then she asks me again, "Chocolate Chip Cookies or Lemon Coconut Cake? Answer me"! The second time she asked me the question I begin to smile and say very softly,"caaaak". She almost went into shock, after all I was in a coma for some time. She ran outside of my room to tell the doctors, but they did not believe her because by the time they got to my room I had slipped back into a deep sleep. I heard her say, "Baby it's going to be all right. God has a work for you to do". Then I began to rest again, only this time it was not in comatose state, I was resting because I was very tired and needed to sleep.

     I was very tired and weak. Shoot, I just had major brain surgery and haven't used any of my muscles or limbs for a month. But every day I stayed awake a little longer, and my mind and my vision were getting much better. It hurt to move though. After lying in bed for a month, I forgot how to move. I could not eat by myself, drink by myself, or go to the bathroom by myself. I would cry every night because I was so helpless. One day the doctors came into my room, like they usually do to check if everything was ok. It was still difficult to move my limbs or to talk or to think since I had awakened. The occupational therapist would come into my room everyday so I could exercise my legs and arms. I would have to lift my legs up as far as I could, which wasn't very far and do the same with my arms. This exercise I guess was to strengthen my muscles and limbs and it wasn't helping very much. I still could not talk, maybe I could nod my head a little but that was about it. Up and down for yes and side to side for no was the way I communicated. Shocked that I was in this condition I began to worry that I would be in this condition for the rest of my life. Although I could not speak I could hear and see. And what I saw around me were doctors constantly checking my vital signs and people around me that either had strokes or brain aneurysms.

There was a lady that whom I shared a room with who also had a stroke. Every time the doctors came in to check her condition there was no change. She lay in her bed immobilized. I began to feel sorry for her because when the doctors would pinch her in different places on her body and, ask her if she felt anything, she would always say no. I on the other hand, who just had a stroke and a brain aneurysm at the same time, was beginning to feel a little sensation in my legs and body. I saw patients riding in the halls in wheelchairs, walking the halls with their IV poles, doctors, nurses oh my. I just wanted to get out of that place! One night I felt as if I had to go to the bathroom so I rang my bell so that the night nurse can bring me a bed pan. I used to pee on myself but slowly I was beginning to recognize the feeling of when I had to use the bathroom. The night nurse entered my room and asked me what he can do for me. I looked at the bed pan, nodded my head up and down signaling I needed to go to the bathroom. The nurse was about 6ft. tall with a dark brown complexion. He wore a short crop afro that was red and, his eyes were blue. Blue? He had to be wearing contact lenses. A black man with blue eyes is a scary sight to see in the middle of the night especially when you can't move or scream. I remember being so afraid that night that I cried while he was putting the bed pan underneath me. I was so afraid that he was going to touch me in a place where he shouldn't and I couldn't fight him, scream or open up my mouth. I felt so humiliated, helpless and afraid that I made myself a promise. I promised myself that come hell or high water, with God's help, I will walk

again, I will talk again and I will go to the bathroom all by

myself again.

Going back to my teenage years, it was not easy going back and forth to school for an additional 5 hours every day traveling from Queen to Brooklyn and from Brooklyn to Queens. I was often hungry and very tired. I was 14 years old and commuting just like a grown up adult. Sometimes I would be so hungry that I would spend my bus fare to buy food, chips or something to eat. I needed more energy, I needed to eat more. Some of the kids I knew at school would buy pizza or subs for lunch and I would join them spending my bus money. I would always get home in the evenings when it was dark outside. Sometimes it seemed as though I would lose track of my days because by the time I got home, did my homework and ate dinner, it would be time for me to go to bed and begin the madness again in the morning. I stared to dread the thought of waking up in the mornings.

It would be cold and dark. I began to think that maybe it wouldn't be a bad to go to the high school in the neighborhood. If I went to the neighborhood school I would have more time to do other things and the people that I meet there will be my friends. If I did that I could spend time at their houses instead of being in mine. There it is! I rationalized everything! I would talk to my mother tonight to see if she would switch my school.

I wasn't very excited about going to a new school but, it was better than commuting every day to Brooklyn and being extremely tired at the end of the day as though I were a Hebrew slave. So one day my mother and I went to transfer me to Bryant High School. To my surprise, as we were sitting in the office waiting, some of the kids that I saw out of our back window smoking weed were in that school. "Oh my God! Yes!" I thought to myself. I couldn't wait to bump into them at school. I was getting excited. May they would allow me to hang out with them just like the kids at the shelter. After my mother took care of my transfer, I couldn't wait to go to school the next day. I was happier than I've been in a long time. New friends, new teachers and, weed smokers, a new location, it almost seemed that I've died and gone on to heaven!

On the first day, to get to the school, I had to ride the bus with the other kids from the projects. I've never saw anything like what I saw on that day. My mother always bought me clothes that were fitting for a young lady. I wore dresses, skirts, pretty blouses because she wanted me to look like a young lady not a street urchin. She would buy me shoes as opposed to sneaker because she believed that sneakers weren't for school, it was just for gym so I only had 1 pair of gym shoes. I wore two piece pant suits adequate and fitting for a girl my age. After all, back in Brooklyn I was a prized possession excelling in academic abilities and a jewel to my family. In other words, she dressed me professionally. Going to the bus stop on my first day in the new school was a culture shock. There were girls wearing jeans and sneakers, they were wearing make-up, they were yelling, cursing and, pushing each other. "What the heck was going on" I thought to myself. And the boys were all wearing their brand new sneakers, baseball caps, hugging different girls and I'm thinking to myself, "If I'm going to fit in I need to remember these things". When I finally made it to class I was disappointed, it was nothing like the school I just came from it was horrible. The classes were overcrowded and there were definitely too many black folk. The other high school was luxurious compared to this place. Edward R. Murrow was a newly built high school with a biology greenhouse, and this place looked like the only green that would be there is marijuana.

After a couple of days, I met a few girls in the lunchroom and found out we all lived in the same neighborhood. They were a rowdy bunch but, I had to fit in somewhere. It's the same as if someone was in prison and had to find that certain click for protection, I had to fit in somewhere. They spoke of cutting class and going into the bathroom and smoking cigarettes. They asked me if I wanted to come along. At first I was nervous but, I shook off my fear and told them yes. I have never cut class before but what the hell it's a new day. I shook off my fear, followed them to the bathroom and when it was my turn to smoke I acted as if I've been smoking my whole life. After we smoked a cigarette one of the girls came up with a plan. The plan she came up with was to hang out in the staircase of the school during classes, wait

for a white girl, beat her up and rob her.

"Oh my God! What did I get myself into?" I

thought to myself. But I couldn't back out because they

would have thought I was a wimp. So again I agreed with

them. We went to the staircase between the second and

third floors and waited. We were waiting for some poor

soul to either be going up or down the staircase to jump

them. They made sure that I knew they had done this

before and that it had to be a girl because boy can be

difficult and powerful. So we waited until we heard

someone coming. Finally there was a sound. A sound of

footsteps coming down the steps toward us. We all had

to be very quiet so that the person could not hear us. As

they were approaching my heart felt as if it were beating

a thousand beats a minute. In the few seconds it took for

the girl to finally reach where we were it seemed as if it were an eternity. She finally reached us. One of the girls asked her where she was going and she said to the office. The homegirl proceeded to tell the white girl that she wasn't going anywhere, all of the sudden she hit the white girl in the face with all of her strength and the girl fell backward. One of the other girls snatched her book bag and her handbag and started to run down the steps. There were four of us, she was outnumbered.

As soon as the others snatched the girl's bags, we began to run down the steps of the staircase, I knew that it was my cue to begin running also. We all ran down the steps and ran out of the side door of the school. Running, panting, sweating, scared. We had just robbed someone on school property. We left her on the steps and ran for our lives. If I got caught my mother would kill me. We ran out of the building and towards the bus stop, the bus that would take us home. But we couldn't stand there, it be too obvious, it was too close to the school. So we ran about 5 blocks to another bus stop so that we wouldn't get caught. Laughing, we thought we were something bad, robbing someone at school. I thought I was bad, invincible and it felt good. I felt powerful for once. The bus finally arrived and we got on it to go home. When the bus arrived in the projects we decided that whatever money was in her bag we would split up amongst us.

There was a whole whopping 10 bucks. Ten bucks!! How were we going to divide ten dollars between 4 people? That would mean that everyone would get $2.50 apiece.

All of that trouble for $2.50 cents! So instead we decided to meet in an hour, we would buy a nickel bag of weed, some beer and a couple of cigarettes. We did all of that work for ten dollars. There has to be more to this life.

My mother never found out what happened on that day but for me it was the beginning of a new life. A new life of crime, a life of drugs, a life of societal disobedience, a life of freedom. Oh let me not forget a life that would keep me away from the house and him. Mom didn't know that I was cutting classes and not going to school. In those days, the attendance letters could come home by mail and I would make sure that I was home to get the mail before my mother so that any correspondence that came from school I can rip up. So what was I doing all day while I wasn't in school? I was hanging out at different people's houses, smoking weed and sleeping. Who cared anyhow? My mother was at work, my siblings were in school and, he was sleeping in the house. No one cared about me and what I was doing anyhow? No one ever took the time to ask me how was my day or how are you doing in school? So my little heart began to get hardened and I began to form my own little world. I made my own world that was full of fantasy, full of fun, full of mischief and safe from being molested in my own home. All I wanted to do was be a little girl but he had to ruin that. Why is he around anyhow?

It was a beautiful day, it was warm, the sun was shining, a great day to go to the movies. My friends and I decided that we would go and see what was playing at the theatre. It's been a long time since I've said anything to him or him to me, so out of desperation I decided to ask him for some money. I wanted a loan just until my mother came home. I asked my friends to come with me to my house so that I can get some money so I could go with them to the movies. As I walked into the house I had second thoughts but, I wanted to go to the movies so bad that I told myself I was going to ask him anyhow. Before I asked him I remembered that I had not eaten so I made myself a bacon and egg sandwich on white toast. After I made my sandwich I put it on a plate and put the plate on the dresser in my room. After I did he came into my room and said, "I see you made yourself a sandwich. You could've made me one too." And he began laughing. His laugh made me feel uncomfortable but I needed that money for the movies. I forced myself to laugh, and then I asked him the question, "Do you think that I can borrow 5 dollars until Ma gets home so that I can go to the movies with my friends?" Again he laughed and said," I'll give you the 5 dollars but, you have to do me a favor Ok"? When he said that my heart dropped, I couldn't believe what I was hearing. For some strange reason I felt as if the favor he was going to ask me was not good. "What's the favor?" I asked. "If you let me suck your titties, I'll give you the 5 dollars and you wouldn't have to pay me back". After he said that to me I grabbed my plate from off of the dresser and smashed it in his face. He tried to grab me but I fought him like a wild tiger. He was more than 6 ft. tall, and well over 200 lbs., but I didn't care. I fought him with everything I had. Tears were streaming down my face, I could not believe what this man just said to me. I was only 14 years old. I fought my way out of his grasp kicking and punching. With tears running down my face I ran into the living room where my friends were waiting for me. I said to them, "Let's go". They asked me what was wrong but, I couldn't find the words to tell them. "Anybody got a joint" I said. "I need to get high."

I was old enough and wise enough to know that something was definitely wrong. After that incident I knew what was happening to me. It didn't feel right because it wasn't right and I did not have to accept it any longer. So after years of being mentally abused I couldn't take it any longer. I had to tell my mother. So that night, when my mother came in from work I decided that come hell or high water I was going to tell her about everything that this man was doing to me over the years.

My mother finally came home from work that night and I told her that I had to talk to her. She wanted me to speak in front of everyone that was home but I told her that what I had to say had to be done in private. We walked to the front door of the apartment where nobody was standing and I began to tell her what happened that day before she came home from work. I also told her about the time he touched me when I was a little girl and how every now and then he would say nasty things to me and look at me in evil ways. At first I thought she would get upset and tell him to get out of the house but, her reaction was the complete opposite. She remained calm, as calm as a cucumber. She called my sister over to us and told her to grab her jacket we were going for a walk. The three of us went outside for a walk; we walked about 5 minutes alongside the East River in silence. The silence was nerve racking, I wished I knew what she was thinking or what she was going to do about that man. When we got to a bench she told us to sit down. She asked me to tell my story again so that my sister could hear it. After I told my story to my sister, she asked her if he tried to approach her or had done anything to her as well. My sister told us that he hadn't. My mother told us that we were going back to the house she had heard enough. When we returned to the house my mother confronted him. I was so happy! Ecstatic is what I was, it seemed as if my heart was going to jump right out of my mouth. My mom is going to tell him off, she's going to kick him out of our lives forever and ever amen! No more living in fear, no more running for me, I will finally feel safe. He's going to leave our home, she was going to put him out of our house. She pulled him to the side away from us to confront him, I guess she did not want us to hear what she was saying to him. Finally, she returned to where my sister and I stood, she looked at us and said, "He said that none of what you said ever happened, he said that it is only your imagination. He said you are in la-la land and you wish that it would've happened. He said you're lying". "No, it's not me Ma! It's him! He's the liar" I yelled out with tears in my eyes. I felt as if the world was dropping from under my feet and my entire body was sinking into hell. "Wash up and go to bed, I don't ever want to hear anything about this ever again!" she said. I was furious, how could she do this to me! He violated me, violated my mind and she believes him? What am I going to do? Where am I going to go to get away from this madness, this insane house? I could do nothing, I had nowhere to go, I didn't have any money. So in my bed I cried, I cried so much I cried myself to sleep.

When I woke up the next morning, I knew that the old Deborah was left crying in her bed the night before. Now it is a new day, now there had to be a new me. I woke up feeling rejected and dirty therefore I had to toughen my skin. I guess love is truly blind. I saw it first hand when she chose his words over mine. Now the cat was out of the bag and I felt so alone but that's not the way it's supposed to be. I felt alienated from my own family. I began to hang out longer to be away from the house. I began to use more marijuana to escape my own thoughts, the demons in my head. I started being very adventurous, going places with others that I would have been afraid to go to before. I was young, pretty, and smart so I began to use those attributes to get what I wanted. Whether it was drugs, food or a place to rest my head I began to use my brain to get what I needed. Although I tried to kill myself at one point by swallowing a whole bottle of pills I didn't die, there was a reason I had to live. In order for me to live I had to get smart. I started not to care about anyone or anything and why should I? No one cared about me! When you can't trust your own mother, the woman that gave birth to you, the woman who supposed to love you, the woman who is supposed to be your role model, if you can't trust your own mother who can you trust? When you can't trust anyone in your house, you begin to trust those who are in the streets. I began to trust my so called friends, the hustlers, the drug dealers, the club owners, the prostitutes the people of the streets. I had to learn the way of the streets in order to survive. And I did.

The streets are a place where there are all kinds of people doing all kinds of things but, the streets that I'm talking about is the streets of the ghetto. Ghetto streets the getaway from reality. The place where fast money is made if you are strong enough because on the streets were also death. Like a lion going after its prey, if you weren't swift enough or smart enough you could get eaten alive. So I had to learn the game in order to survive. Something inside of me didn't want to play the street game, I really didn't want to be in the streets but I didn't really have a choice. My choices were to be in a house where there was no trust, manipulation, abuse and anger or, find a new path in life on the streets where people could relate to what I was feeling so I thought.

Still something inside of me did not want to play the game. I wanted to be home in a warm and loving house. I guess I was looking for someone that I could trust and they could trust me in return. Someone that would give me the love that I deserved and I would love them in return. I needed for someone to love me, a place to call home, somewhere where I could feel secure. Looking and searching, searching and looking. Anywhere, everywhere and I won't give up until I find it. I know it's out there somewhere. I chose to hang out with people who were older me. They've been playing this game longer than I have, with age comes wisdom and they knew the ropes. Many of the girls my age that I knew weren't in the same predicament I was in so I didn't hang out with them much. I had to learn how to make money on the streets and fast. Of course when you start out you need protection.

I befriended a woman who seemed to the streets very well. She came from a big family, all of whom sold drugs but, she was different she had protection. She had children, she sold drugs and ran the numbers game. I didn't have any children but I wanted to be just like her. She seemed confident, she made money and no one messed with her. One day she needed a babysitter while she went to pick up some drugs and I just happened to be available. "How much will you pay me if I watched your kids for you" I asked her. She told me she would pay me twenty dollars if I watched them for an hour. I told her I would do it. That was the first time that I made money on the street but, I knew that if I could get closer to her she would teach me everything that she knew and she did. She began to trust me, she showed me how to take numbers and I started making money. Everything was fine for a while until her boyfriend started to talk to me, pay attention to me. We would be joking around and I could feel her eyes staring at us. One day she accused me of trying to flirt with her man. She told me she didn't want me around anymore. It was fine with me though because by that time I was able to build up my own contacts. People who was a step higher than she was, people that sold way more drugs and, had way more money than she did. If I was going to play the game, I had to step up my game. I'm pretty, smart and willing to take chances so I can do better than this nickel and dime bitch. She did me a favor by dismissing my services, now I can use the skills that I have to further my criminal career.

There was a man who came around once in a while to sell heroin in the projects. When he came around it was like being in the movies, it was like being in a scene from "Cotton Comes to Harlem" or "Superfly". He was young, handsome and had a nice car. Everyone would flock around him as though he was giving away money. When he came around he would park his car near a spot where everyone was hanging out and get out of his car holding two shopping bags. At first I thought he was the neighborhood Robin Hood who came around to give away food and clothes, only to find out that there was heroin in the shopping bags. I was amazed at the respect that was given to him by the people; there were old people around him and young people as well. I found out that some of the people that were around him were waiting to get their new package of heroin. I want what he has, the respect and money. I had to get next to him. If I could get to know him all of my troubles would be over. I made it my business to hang around just as the others did when he came on the block. His family lived in the neighborhood so I can find out who they are and get friendly with them. I've been learning how to manipulate situations to get what I want. I became friends with his brother who was a heroin junkie. He thought that I liked him and wanted to spend time with him when all along I wanted to get to know his brother. One day we were sitting in his living room listening to music and talking when his brother came into the apartment. WOW!! It was the perfect opportunity, the opportunity that I waited so long for. It was like a dream come true, no hustler can resist a pretty face of a street smart young lady who hangs out with a junkie. His brother introduced us to each other and we connected. He gave me his phone number, just what I was hoping for. Bingo!! We began talking on the phone at night, going on dates mostly late at night. We started to get to know each other better. He knew that I wanted some excitement in my life, including the desire to make money on the street so he propositioned me. He needed someone to sit in this bar in the Bronx, with him there of course, to hold drugs for him and he would pay them. He asked me if I would do it. "Of course" I replied. It was time to start making some real money. And all I would have to do is sit there and what he told me to do just do it. I really thought I was smart, I didn't realize that it was a set-up for me to sell and handle the heroin at the bar without him being there.

After a couple of days of sitting in the bar with him close by he told me he had another spot that he had to take care of and needed me to go to the bar by myself. He said I wouldn't have to worry about anybody bothering me because everyone knew him and now they knew me. I knew who the customers were, that wasn't a problem, and I can sit at the bar and just deal drugs. I would spend a couple of hours there from about 4pm until about 12am and I would make $150 dollars a day.

Who wouldn't grab an opportunity like that at the age of

fifteen? I thought that I was all that and a bag of chips!

Not knowing at the time that I was being set up to live a

life full of deceit and that could result in death.

After that, I began to get myself deeper and

deeper into the life of crime and drugs. By the age of

seventeen I was selling heroin and using cocaine, not to

mention drinking and smoking. I vowed that I would not

be like my father who was a heroin junkie so I

experimented with every drug that I could get my hands

on. Although I sniffed dope I never shot dope. That was

my father's thing so I never did it. It gave me an excuse to

say I wasn't like him although one day my mother told me

that I not only looked like him but, I acted like him also.

I've experimented with speed, acid, snorted heroin and

cocaine and at times mixed the two into a speedball. Instead of selling the dope, I started using it. I snorted so much pure heroin one morning I woke up to a warm liquid running down my nose. It was blood pouring out of my nostrils because of putting that junk in my nose. That was the last time I sniffed heroin but, I still continued to use other drugs. Because of my drug use and popularity among addicts, heroin addicts did not have a problem shooting up their drugs in front of me. Heck at times they offered to help me shoot up.

A Spanish guy bought 2 bags of dope off of me. He wanted to get high but he didn't have anywhere to go that was safe enough to shoot up. We decided I would be his lookout and we would go into the back staircase of a nearby building where he can shoot up his drugs. We went into the back staircase of a building, making sure no one was there; he pulled out his syringe and needle that was in his jacket pocket. While he was getting ready to get high we were having an intelligent conversation. Talking about people around the block, what was going on in the news etc. People who are addicted are not stupid it's just that their priorities are mixed up. While he was putting the rubber band around his arm, tightening it until a vein popped up, I can feel my adrenaline flowing. I'm getting excited watching this man preparing to get high. He seemed to be excited also. This man is smiling, laughing and sweating all at the same time. He taps his arm where the band was to make sure that the vein is puffed up and ready for the dope. He sticks the needle into his vein carefully with precision like an artist with his paintbrush preparing to draw a masterpiece. He pushes the top of the syringe just a little allowing the liquid inside to slowly travel down the syringe into the needle where it will enter the vein. Then he draws back on the syringe and mixes his blood with the liquid substance inside of the tube. Although I am not shooting up, a sense of euphoria runs through my entire body as I watch him. He pushes the syringe down again to fill his vein with some more of the smack but, this time he pushes the rest of the liquid in his arm and his head begins to tilt backward. The heroin is going straight into his bloodstream where it can engulf him at lightning speed. His head moves from the position of being backward with his eyes closed to facing me and then he stops short. He looks at me terrified, confused and in shock. He couldn't speak, words were forming from his mouth but there wasn't any sound. "What the hell is going on" I screamed. Then it dawned on me. The man was overdosing on the drug. He was overdosing on heroin in the back staircase! Oh my God!! Why me? Why now? What am I going to do? Do I leave him here and let him die? Do I call the ambulance? If I call the ambulance I can't be here. Jesus!! I have to help

him but, what can I do? So I stuck my fingers down his

throat to make him throw up. I heard somewhere that if

you do that to a person who is overdosing it may help

them to recover. At first he wouldn't throw up but, I kept

stuffing my fingers down this throat until he did.

Eventually he threw up but when he did I ran. I ran out of

the building to a pay phone, I called the police and told

them that there was a man overdosing off of heroin in the

back stairwell of the building. I watched the building from

across the street until the cops and the ambulance got

there. They took him out on a stretcher and I thought

that he had died, but he didn't die. I saw him a couple of

days later on the block buying some more drugs. I never

went near that man again. Dummy!

I started smoking crack cocaine I heard that is was better and safer than using heroin. I didn't want to use heroin anyhow, that's what my father did. I would constantly tell myself that he shot up heroin so I never would not realizing that no matter what drug I used I was beginning to be like him. That is one of the reasons why we have to be so careful of what we say to our children. I remember my mother saying to me that I looked like my father and acted like him too. So why not go all the way and be an addict like he was. At first it was great! Smoking crack gave me a high like no other high I gotten before. It made me feel invincible, alert, like I can do anything I put my mind to. Not knowing that for years after I would be chasing that first high. One night I went to hang out in Harlem, 145th street and St. Nicholas Avenue because I knew that they big time hustlers and money makers were there. Harlem was the place where you can go if you wanted a good bag of dope. It was also

the place you can go to get some of the best cocaine or

crack if that's what you wanted you just needed to know

who to talk to or where to go. I knew this spot on 145th

Street, a club that was open all night. This place was

where the real crack smokers hung out. When you

walked in the joint there were tables, chairs and different

sections that a person can go to smoke their drugs and

get high. Everywhere you looked people were either

getting high or were already high. Whatever you needed

was supplied right there. There were crack pipes for sale,

lighters, and stems and if you ran out of crack there was a

dealer right there at your fingertips.

As I entered the place I looked around at the

faces of the people who were there to see if I recognized

anybody. I was glad when I saw someone that I knew. As

a matter of fact, the person that I saw was one of my partners. We used to go to different gambling clubs and cheat people out of their money playing 21 Blackjack until we were chased and shot at when they caught us cheating that day. I was glad to see a familiar face because we could talk and get high at the same time. At 4:00 am I was ready to go home, my money had ran out, I was tired of sucking on the pipe and soon it was going to be daylight. I asked him what time he was leaving so I could get a ride back home. I didn't know exactly where he lived but I knew that he didn't live far from where I did. He said he would take me home. What a relief! I wouldn't have to take a cab home or take the train in my condition. About a half an hour later we were leaving the club and on our way to go home. I enjoyed the ride, over the Tri-Boro Bridge in the wee hours of the morning while the sky is turning from darkness to light. As we exited the expressway I knew that I would be home soon.

As I was looking out of the window of the car I can see that churches are open after all its Sunday morning. I see families dressed up on their way to church. There were mothers, fathers and children holding hands on their way to give God thanks in the sanctuary.   I began to wonder why wasn't I going to church, they looked so happy, but instead I'm high out of my mind because I was smoking crack all night. On the way home, very close to my house, was a big Catholic Church with stained glass windows, a bell tower that rung when mass was beginning and when mass was over and, a very tall steeple that almost reached the clouds. Just as I was staring out of the window at the people he stops the car, I turned my head to face him wondering why we stopped. "Get out of the car! You're coming with me" he said. Fear raced through my heart, my mind, and my soul because

he had a gun pointing directly in my face. This is not

happening! If I don't do what he says he's going to kill me!

Kill me right here in front of this church! Oh my God! I'm

facing the devil! What am I going to do? If I go with him

he'll rape me and probably still kill me. Tears began to

flow down my face, I was so scared, helpless but I had to

think quickly because if I didn't my life was going to end

right here at that very moment. I was so scared and

shakin up that I wasn't high any more. I had to think

quickly. His car had those automatic locks on the doors,

he must've forgotten he unlocked them for me to get out

when he told me too. I had to think quickly, If I don't he's

going to kill me right here, right now. I don't know why I

did it but I did, I made eye to eye contact with the devil to

hopefully divert and distract his thinking. If I can do that

and he falls for it then I can take my left hand, push the

gun out of my face, then push the car door open and run like holy hell into the church. If my thoughts are correct he will not enter the church because he's surely a demon. There's not much time, I have to move! So I looked at him eyeball to eyeball and he stared back at my eyeball to eyeball. We stared at each other for about 10 seconds which seemed to be the longest 10 seconds of my life. Something inside of me said, "NOW"! So I threw up my left hand against the hand that he was holding the pistol with, it flew into the backseat of the car. Now is my break!! As he tried to retrieve the gun, I opened the door of the car and ran up the steps of the church screaming at the top of my lungs," He's going to kill me. Help! Somebody please help me! He's trying to kill me"! People's heads flung around to see what was going on. There were some people who were waving me along, and some people were holding the church doors open so that

I can run inside. Sanctuary!! People were screaming,
"What's going on". I told them that there was a man that
was trying to kill me. They told me I would be safe inside
and when he was gone I could leave if I wanted to. But
every time I looked outside to see if he was gone he was
still outside. He was still waiting right outside the church
for me to come out. Occasionally, I would peep outside
of the big church doors to make sure I didn't see him and I
did. Finally, at one point I peeped outside to see if he was
still there and he was gone. I could leave my sanctuary
and walk home it wasn't very far or, I could wait for the
bus. I waited until I saw the bus coming then I ran outside
of the church to get on it. Wheww I was safe now. I
began to relax a little on the bus, saying good morning to
some of the people on it trying to keep my composure.
The bus reached my destination and I was going to finally
make it home.

I was finally safe, as was looking out of the window of the bus there he was. Oh my God! The devil would not come inside the church but waited for me to come out. I became frantic, scared all over again. What am I going to do? I can't get off of this bus ever! It was the last stop on the Q102 bus it was time for everyone to get off of the bus, but I couldn't and I wouldn't get off of the bus. There was a woman who was getting off and noticed that I was stricken with panic. She asked me what was wrong. Breathing heavily I told her the story of the man that was trying to kill me. By this time he was out of his car approaching the bus. He walked up the steps of the bus and told the bus driver that I was his little sister who ran away from home. Thank God someone on the bus knew me and spoke up on my behalf. She told the driver that I was not his sister. The driver told that demon of a man," If you don't get off of this bus right now I'm

going to call the police". That man gave me an evil look,

and then he turned around and got off of the bus. I

couldn't get off of the bus and go home now so, I decided

to ride the bus until I got to the train station and went to

the Bronx. When I finally got off of the bus at the station

he was nowhere to be seen. But that episode did not

stop me from living foolishly. Two weeks later there was a

story about him in the New York Post. Apparently he was

cheating in a card game up in Harlem and someone shot

him in the head. He was dead.

My careless way of living didn't stop there, I felt

as though I cheated death. I was invincible. My mother

said I was uncontrollable because I would come home in

the wee hours of the morning most of the time high. I

would be out all night gambling, hustling, drinking and

using drugs. I believe that my mother knew I wasn't going to school because on this particular morning I overslept and she kept trying to wake me so that I can leave the house before she went to work. She kept pushing me and shoving me to get out of my bed but, I kept ignoring her. Finally I went back to sleep. A little while later, I heard the voices of strange men in my room. "Miss, get up and get dressed. You're coming with us" they said. That didn't sound like my mother, or her boyfriend. I opened my eyes to see two policemen standing over me telling me I had to go with them. I looked at my mother for some type of explanation but, she turned the other way looking up at the ceiling. They said they would give me 5 minutes to put on my clothes and go with them. I looked at my mother again and all she could say to me is do as you're told. The police took me to family court. My mother had taken out a PINS (person in need of supervision) warrant against me because I was out of control, not going to school and very disrespectful towards her and my entire family. When we went to court the judge wanted to put me in a juvenile group home but, being that we had a Catholic background he allowed me to go to a home for girls upstate in New York. The facility was called Graymoor Manor, it was a residential group home for girls with behavioral problems. My situation must have been really crazy because at Graymoor the staff consisted of priests and nuns who conducted the group therapy sessions. All day long, everywhere I looked I saw nuns in habits and priests in robes and collars. At one point I thought they were going to do an exorcism on me. Father Egan was the priest in charge of the whole facility, he was known as the "Junkie Priest". He was named that because he had written a book called "Junkie Priest", he used to be a junkie.

I was in Graymoor for about a year when I was allowed to visit home. I had to take a chaperone with me because I was not trusted to be alone especially when I was going back to my old neighborhood. I chose to take a girl with me home who was older than I and was in Graymoor longer than I've been. She seemed a little bit naïve; I think I was a bit smarter so I chose her. When I finally went on my home visit, everyone was so happy to see me. My family prepared a big party with some of my old friend and family, it reminded me of the parties that are given to people who just got out of jail. But all I wanted to do is get high. I've been away for a while and that crack was calling my name. I told my mother that I wanted to visit someone who lived across the hall from us and I would be right back. Of course she didn't trust me and neither did the girl who I bought with me home. And why should they, I didn't trust myself either. They spoke against me going across the hall but I convinced them that I would be right back. Guess what? They let me go free. My adrenaline began rushing because I knew that once I walked out the apartment doors I was not coming back. I opened the front door as if I was going to the neighbor's house; I turned around to make sure no one was following me. No one was following me so, I quickly opened up the stairwell door, ran down the steps and out of the building to freedom. A freedom from people telling me what to do, freedom from people telling me how to act, freedom from priests, nuns and freedom from Graymoor. A freedom to get high once again, freedom to run the streets. Freedom to return back to my sanctuary.

I was not going back home, I was not going back to Graymoor but, I needed a place to live. I would live in the street I told myself, someone would take me in and let me stay with them for a while. Someone would have pity on a young girl who could not go home because of an abusive stepfather. There had to be someone that can help me. I thought that someone would but, nothing in the streets come without a price. So I got deeper into the mess. I needed money so I began working in local bars as a barmaid, getting high and watching the Go-Go dancers dance and do unmentionable things for a buck.

When I officially left home at the age of 17 I lived on the street. Staying here, staying there. I was living as if I was a nomad; I was living anywhere and everywhere as long as I didn't have to live in that house with that man who was my mother's boyfriend. After living like that for about 3 years a friend of mine offered me a place to stay for a while. She lived with her mother mostly but, she had her own apartment in Queensbridge Housing. After about a year of working in the bar and hustling, I decided to go back to school to get my GED. Around the time I finished my classes and passed the test for my GED, I was pregnant with my first son. I moved out of my girlfriend's house to live with my "Baby Daddy" and his family. I thought he really cared about me but, he really didn't. I found out that while I was living with him, getting ready to have his child, he was cheating on me with another girl. I vowed that I would not let another man take advantage of me as long as I lived. So after my son was born I moved out into a room in Brooklyn. One night my mother kept my son overnight so that I can go home and get some rest because I had to work the next morning. I remember going home to Brooklyn and walking from the train station to my house when someone on a bicycle pulled up alongside of me asking what time it was. I looked down at my watch, looked up at him to tell the time, but when I looked up there was a gun in my face and he said," You know what time it is". Oh no not again! Another gun in my face! He demanded that I give him my money. I had $70 dollars in my pocket which I had just won shooting dice before I went to Brooklyn. I went into my pocket and gave it all to him. He was getting ready to ride off on his bike, when I said to him, "Look! You just took all of my money. I have to go to work tomorrow so can you give me $3 dollars back"? I was surprised when he said ok. Then he got off of his bike and told me to take all of my clothes off. "Are you kidding me? You just took all of my money and now you want me to take my clothes off too?" "Ok, ok never mind" he said, and then he rode off on his bike. I was so shaken up that I ran up the steps to my house, locked the doors once I was inside, prayed and went to sleep. The next day I reported the robbery and found out I wasn't the only person who had. There had been reports of a man riding around on a bicycle robbing women at gunpoint in the Brownsville section of Brooklyn.

For years afterward I continued to smoke crack cocaine. I couldn't hold a decent job or any job because of my addiction. I would enter 28 day programs periodically but they would never work for me. As soon as the 28 days were over I would wind up back on the street looking for some crack. By this time I had 3 children, two of whom were fathered by a drug dealer. I left one day to go to the store and left them with their father. When I didn't come back for a couple of hours, because I found my way to the crack house, he began to circulate my picture in the neighborhood in hopes that someone would recognize me. He offered a reward of

$100 dollars to anyone that could lead him to me. I stayed away from home getting high for hours with no one knowing where I was. It was about 3:00 am when there was a knock on the door of the crack house. Someone answered the door, turned to me and said there was someone at the door looking for me. My heart started pounding because at the door was my children's father and the man who sold me out for the $100 dollars. When a person is a crack addict everything means nothing. Your children mean nothing, your boyfriend, your mother, your grandmother mean nothing at all. The only thing that mattered was me putting my lips on that glass pipe and watching my life go up in a cloud of smoke. He handed the man the $100 dollars, held out his hand for me to hold it and, he said lets go. I was scared to death as we walked home in silence. When we got to the apartment I thought I was safe. He found me and that was that. I believed he really cared about me because no one else would pay someone to find their children's mother. He was saving me from myself and the people in the crack house. Someone had to save me because I can't save myself I don't know how. We turned into the kitchen, he held my arm gently and turned me around to him, we were looking into each other's eyes and I was waiting for him to kiss me, to love me. He continued to stare at me and then with all the power he could muster up, he balled up his fist and hit me so hard in the face I fell to the floor. There was blood everywhere! I was screaming and crying, "Help! Help! Please somebody help me!" but no one came. As I lay on the floor crying he started to kick me in my stomach, on my back. I thought I was going to die. When he finally stopped, as I lay in blood, he bent down and snatched off my pants. Not only did he beat the shit out of me but, he raped me.

Although I didn't deserve to be treated like that, at the time I thought I deserved it. Did I call the police? No I did not. He sold drugs and I used drugs so who would believe me. I was nobody but a crackhead.

My children were taken away from me by the family court and the court gave my Aunt temporary custody of them. I was mandated to go into a drug rehabilitation program for 18 months. Upon completion of the program if I obtained adequate housing and a job I can regain custody of my children. I had absolutely nothing. My family turned their backs on me, my children were taken away from me so I went into the program. I can't keep living this way or else I'm going to die. Someone referred me to a place called named the Delancy Street Foundation. This program was not like your typical Daytop Village or government 28 day programs, this program did not have a lot of advertisement. The only advertisement for this program was by word of mouth. I had gotten the telephone number of Delancy Street and called them up. I was told that if I were truly ready to stop using that I can come to them that night, do not bring any clothes or drugs. It wasn't a guarantee that I would be accepted in the program because I had to have an interview consisting of my peers and would determine if I was accepted or not. After the phone call I went to my mother's house and knock on the door. She answer the door but would not let me in, she talked to me through the peephole. I was not allowed to enter into her house for years. I told her about what the people said on the phone and that I wanted to go up there tonight. I told her that I've had enough and wanted my children back. She told me she would meet me at Penn Station, she would put me on the train to go to the program. She met me, bought my train

ticket and when it was time for the train to take off I saw

the tears in her eyes. I love my mother, I always have and

I always will.

I went through the interview process and was

accepted into the therapeutic community, Delancy Street.

I had absolutely nothing. The clothes that I was wearing

were thrown away and I was given new clothes to wear.

Because of my drug addiction and living on the street my

speech was horrific. I could not speak normally nor speak

full sentences. As time when on while I was in the

program I learned to speak properly, think rationally and

obtain marketable skills. It took a while though because

for years I've been using drugs so nothing was going to

change overnight but, I knew that it would change. It

would mean making some tough decisions on my part if I

wanted to recover or not. One thing that was very

exceptional about Delancy Street was that the doors were

always open and a person could walk out at any time if

they wanted to. One time things got really tough and I

wanted to leave, but I didn't. I was glad I didn't because

my life was really beginning to change for the better.

Twice a week we had group counseling sessions

but, twice during a person's stay at Delancy Street they

had to complete one 24 hour dissipation and, one 72 hour

dissipation. The first one was to prepare you for the

second one if a person even stayed that long. The 24

hour dissipation took place in the middle of an eighteen

month stay, and the other took place right before a

person graduated from the program. We sat around in a

circle facing each other, a group of 10 or more individuals

who entered the program around the same time were

part of that specific group. Food was prepared and set on tables. Coffee, water, juice and snacks were set out in case anyone got hungry. During the dissipations no one was allowed to go anywhere but to the bathroom. Present at the dissipations were some of the big shots from the main facility in San Francisco.

The Delancy Street Foundation had 5 facilities nationwide. One in San Francisco, one in New Mexico, the third one was in Los Angeles, another in North Carolina and lastly New York. The founder of the program lived in San Francisco where most of the administration was. Every time that a dissipation was about to happen, no matter what facility it is going to take place at, psychologists and ex-addicts who graduated the program were participants to help us along the way. During the dissipation every person, excluding the doctor and graduates, must tell their life's story. They had to go back as far as they could remember and tell the group. Every

hurt, every good experience, every traumatic experience,

where you got your name from, anything that you could

remember you told the group. I began when I was a little

girl remembering when my biological father used to make

circles when he blew out the smoke of his cigarette. I

spoke about the last time I saw my father when my

mother and he were fighting. She had an iron in her hand

yelling at him and he had a butcher knife threatening her.

I spoke about my stepfather who touched me in my

private parts when I was little and how he mentally

abused me until I was about 15 years old. I told the group

many things including my drug addiction, my children

being taken away, how I hustled and lived on the streets,

people I have hurt and how I've been hurting myself. I

rarely spoke of any good times because to tell you the

truth I hardly remember any. All the while I was crying,

sometimes screaming reliving each and every experience over and over. Just about everything I could remember. Everyone and everything coming back to me clouding my mind and coming back to life. I spoke about the pain, the horror, the feelings, the dirtiness, the disappointments, and the ugliness.   The confusion in my life, the depression, how I tried to kill myself, the unforgiveness I had inside of me. All of the hatred I had for myself coming to the forefront as I speak to these people spilling my guts, telling my story in hopes that going through this hell would help me to never use drugs again. I don't remember how long I spoke for but what I do know is that it was for at least two hours or longer.

After I had told the story of all the years of drug use and abuse, all the years of living the street life it all boiled down to one thing. I needed to forgive my stepfather for what he had done to me when I was a child. What?!! Forgive him? How could I ever forgive the man that tore my family apart, used and abused me mentally and physically! How can I forgive that monster, that devil! With tears rolling down my face, yelling and screaming, "No, I won't ever forgive him for what he's done to me. I hate him! He's the reason why I'm the way that I am! My life would have been different if he never came around. He destroyed me". Some of the staff in the room were professionals therefore after each person told their story they gave their professional opinions of what that person needed to do to get better. I was told in order for me to go on with my life I had to forgive him for what he did to me. They asked me to imagine him sitting next to me and tell him that I forgave him for everything that he did to me. I couldn't do it. All I could do is stare at everyone in the room, but in my mind I was saying, "These people are crazy, I wanna get high". Again they explained to me that I had to forgive him and let go of all the hurt, pain and confusion and for touching me when I was a little girl. If I didn't do it I would be bound to the past not being able to move into my future.

They told me I would be trapped, I would continue to use drugs and destroy everyone I came in contact with including myself. We make choices in this life we can chose to forgive or we cannot forgive and have a mindset that is destructive and can cause death. I thought about my options. I can chose to forgive him and the others who have hurt me or stay stuck in unforgiveness. I choose to try this thing called forgiveness. So I began to scream to an imaginary person sitting next to me, "I FORGIVE YOU"! Everyone started clapping, "I FORGIVE YOU"! Oh my God what is happening to me? "I forgive everyone who has ever hurt me, oh God I forgive, I forgive"! As the tears rushed down my face, shaking my head back and forth, while everyone was clapping and crying along with me, I felt something beginning to lift out of my soul. It was as if a spirit of some sort was beginning to leave my body. I began to feel as light as a feather, floating in the summer air, all of the sudden I could breathe. My sense of smell became acute, the clapping no longer sounded like thunder but sounded like loud applauses, like the angels in heaven were giving me a standing ovation. I can hear angels saying, "Glory to God in the highest. She did it! She did it".

The process has finally begun. I was told that what was done to me at a young age was not my fault, not only must I forgive him but I must start to forgive myself. For years I believed that everything that happened to me was my fault, I made him touch me, I made him say those nasty things to me. Instead of my beauty and intelligence being a blessing it became a curse. All of those years I thought that it was my fault. Now I understand that it wasn't my fault and my healing can begin. After that moment I wanted to live and not die.

I stayed in Delancy Street for 2 ½ years as opposed to the 18 months that the judge had mandated me to be there. I stayed because just like some of the other graduates, I wanted to help newcomers coming into the program. During my stay I learned how to speak better and obtained some marketable skills. I no longer spoke in broken sentences. I could speak proper English and communicate effectively. Before a person leaves the program they must have a job and a place to live. Three months before I graduated and left Delancy Street I started working in a company in Chappaqua NY that sold EEG machines for hospitals as a purchasing secretary. Now that the job was secure I had to find a place to live.

My family knew of a church in the Bronx that had a rooming house where some of the single women in the church lived. It was called the "Girls House" on Grand Avenue. I didn't really want to go there but I didn't have a choice. If I wanted to leave Delancy Street and get my children back so I had to move there.

I arrived at the Girls House with boxes and bags, one of the residents greeted me at the door then she helped me inside the house. She proceeded to give me a tour of the house. It was a two story house in the middle of Grand Avenue in the Bronx. On the first floor there was a kitchen, living room and two bedrooms in the back of the house. On the second floor were more bedrooms and a bathroom. My room would be upstairs. It was a quaint little room with a twin sized bed and a dresser. I was told I could fix it up however I wanted to. I was also told that the curfew time was 10pm, I was told the dinner time and the fellowship schedule. "Fellowship? What's a fellowship?" I asked. "Oh, it's when we all meet up in the living room and talk, we have Bible study, sing and have prayer" she said. Bible study and Prayer? I wanted to run out the door and never look back but I couldn't. I was so tired of running, I had to face this thing head on. "Ok" I said. "And church starts at 10:00 am on Sunday mornings" she said. What!! I had to go to church too! "Great!" I replied but I was fuming inside.

Later that night I met the other women who lived in the house. There was an older woman and her teenage daughter living in one of the rooms, they were waiting for an apartment I guess. In the room next to them was a single woman in her late twenties. Upstairs was another single female and I occupied the last bedroom. I found out that night that the owner of the house was also the

Pastor of the church and he and his family lived next door

in another house on Grand Avenue. They had opened up

the Girls House to help women who needed a place to live

with stipulations of course. One of the stipulations was

that they must attend fellowship and go to church on

Sunday otherwise they would be asked to leave.

Sunday morning came so fast! It's time to get up,

get dressed and go to church. This would be the first time

I've been in a church in years. The last time I was in a

church was when that man put the gun in my face and I

got away. I wasn't sure how to dress but, I was told that I

could wear jeans because God wasn't looking at my

outward appearances he was looking at my heart. That

sounded great because when I was younger in the

Catholic Church I had to dress up. To hear I could wear

jeans was ok with me. As we walked to the church, which wasn't far from the Girls House, it felt good walking on the streets of the Bronx and not being high or having to look behind my shoulder afraid that someone was coming after me. We walked about 5 blocks and there it was Joy Fellowship Church. What kind of name was Joy Fellowship? I'm used to St. Thomas Aquinas or Our Lady of something or other. Later on I found out that the church was a non-denominational church and anyone was welcome. What a relief, no priests and nuns there, God only know I had my share of them. I was glad to be there because my aunt and uncle were there along with my two sons. When I was mandated to go into a program by the court, my relatives had taken custody of my boys and my cousin took custody of my daughter until I got clean. I was so happy to see everyone even if I could only see my children at church. Until I got an apartment of my own, I could not regain custody of my boys. It hurt that I couldn't have them with me but if I stayed clean and got an apartment in no time we would be back together again. This church was quite different than the church I used to go to. People were friendly and smiling, they weren't stoic and stiff-necked like the people in the Catholic Church. They had musicians, there was singing, and people were clapping their hands and dancing. There was a man who went up to the front of the church, he opened up the Bible and began to teach from it. Everyone seemed so happy, it was amazing! I've never seen people so happy before. There were white folk, black folk and Spanish folk all having the time of their lives together. I was in awe! Even my sons, who were about 4 and 6 years old, were singing the church songs. Wow!! When this man went up to the front of the church and began teaching, he kept speaking about a man named Jesus. Jesus this and Jesus that. Jesus, Jesus, Jesus. I kept looking around to see if I saw this Jesus he was talking so much about, but I didn't know what he looked like. I have to find out who this Jesus guy is because the way he is talking about him it sounds like someone I'd like to meet. At the end of the service the people were asked, "If anyone wants Jesus to come into their heart and change their lives, come up to the alter and we will pray with you." I saw people going up to the front of the church for prayer but I didn't. Although I wanted to I didn't budge.

As time went on living in the Girls House, I started to look forward to going to fellowship with the other women. We would cook together at times, sometimes we would go out to the movies, basically have fun without the use of drugs. I was able to go to work commuting to my job everyday by the way of the Metro-North train. The best part was that I was able to spend time with my sons on the weekends. I did have a boyfriend, someone I had been dating while in Delancy Street. We often talked about getting married when he graduated from the program. He was from San Francisco. I had graduated the program before he did so we made a pact that when he finished we would hook up and move out to California. The plan was for me to work in San Francisco and when we accumulated enough money I would send for my boys. His family was very prominent so they would help support us until we got on our feet. Well, that day finally came and it was time to let everyone know that I was leaving the Bronx and moving to California. I was going to get married and send money for my sons to join me there. Some people were against it but, it was my decision to make.

When I arrived in San Francisco he picked me up and took me to our new apartment. I was in awe of the hills, the weather and being on the West coast because I've never been on that side of the United States before. It was a very long trip on the plane, it took 6 hours in the air to get there. Being that his family was very well off, they had already set up a fully furnished apartment for us, which we didn't have to pay any rent for 6 months. They bought us a brand new car, and a job was put into place for me when I arrived.

Life was good for about 6 months when one day, after work we were supposed to meet some friends from Delancy Street San Francisco for dinner and he didn't show up. We waited for about 30 minutes when I decided to call home to see if everything was ok. He answered the phone at home, assured me that everything was ok and that he would be there soon. Again we waited and he did not show up. Finally I apologized and told them that I was going home. I arrived at the apartment, walked in and called his name. No one answered. I sat on the couch, reached out to the coffee table to grab the remote and turn the television on but the remote wasn't on the table. So I got up off of the couch to walk over to the TV and turn it on but, the TV was gone. Oh my God, we've been robbed! I began to look around the house to see if anything else was missing, nothing was missing just the TV. While I was getting ready to pick up the phone to call the police he walked in the door. As I'm telling him about the robbery he is in shock. He assured me that he would call his father who is a judge and he will straighten this whole mess out and find the ones who did this. The police came to the house and questioned us and wrote a police report.

A couple of days afterward, another incident occurred. As I walked into the apartment, after working all day, I smelled something I haven't smelled in a long time, the smell of body odor and dried up urine, it was a horrible smell. "No he did not bring some homeless person into this house"! When he finally came home I questioned him about the smell. He said that his buddy came to the house for a little while and needed to shower. Something was not beginning to feel right. Other things were beginning to happen such as; money missing out of my pocketbook and when I asked about it he would say I must've lost it. One night the microwave disappeared while I was at the grocery store, also he sold the car to some people one night and told them to go to the apartment so that I could give them the keys. When they came to pick up the keys, which I didn't have, I told them he scammed them because I didn't have any keys to give to them. They were furious. After that incident I knew that something was definitely wrong, I started to think he started using drugs again.

I started getting scared. I was all the way across the country living with a man who I thought I knew but didn't. I can't allow myself to stay in this situation any longer, I've been clean for 3 years and I can't allow myself to fall and use drugs again. I had to plan an escape, but where can I run to? I can't go back to the Girls House. Maybe I can go back to my mother's house? I've been clean for some time now. Yes she will let me stay with her for a while if I asked her. So I called my mother and asked her if I could stay with her for a little while, just until I got another job and then I would move out. I asked her to allow me 3 months in the house, she agreed upon the 3 months. Now I have to get back to New York without him finding out, but I have to call his parents and let them know that I will be leaving. I called them to tell them what I was planning to do. They thought that it would be best that I went back to New York. About an hour later someone was knocking at the door, I had just gotten out of the shower so I did not have time to dress properly so I answered the door with a towel around me. When I opened the door there were three policemen standing outside of it. I asked them how can I help them but, they pushed past me and began to search the house. One detective said to me that they were looking for him and he heard that I was leaving that night going back to New York. News travels fast! It was to be expected though because his father was a big judge in the town. After they left the apartment I called his father and he bought me an airplane ticket to go back to New York on the Red Eye from San Francisco that night.

I was on the plane from San Francisco to New York arriving at 6am in LaGuardia Airport. LaGuardia was not far from my mother's house in Queens so I caught a taxi from the airport there. I didn't have much luggage because I had left most of my clothes in California. When I got to the house, one of my siblings opened the door for me, I was so happy to be back. It's been years since I've been home. It was about 7:00 am and everyone was still asleep so, I went into the empty bedroom and did the same, I went to sleep. Around 11am my mother and stepfather came into the room and woke me up. They were getting ready to go out and wanted to speak to me before they did. My mother spoke to me, she said, "We've discussed you staying here but maybe that isn't the right decision. When you get up you need to call your brother in the Bronx and ask him if you can stay with him.

We're on our way out". What?! "You told me to come home, get myself out of that situation and now you're saying I can't stay here"? "I'm sorry but, that's our final decision" she said. What could I say to her? I knew that he had persuaded her to not allow me to stay in the house. I know he talked her out of letting me feel safe and secure once again. Once again I felt helpless, hopeless and rejected. I wanted to get high again, it's time to get high. People are taught in most drug programs that a person has to remove himself from people, places and things in order to get strong and stop using, but if you want to get high you know exactly where those people, places and things are and you will find it. I had $300 dollars in my pocket, enough money to kill myself with. Enough money to get as high as the sky, and that is exactly what I was going to do. Who cares about me anyhow? My sons are fine with my aunt, my mother doesn't give a shit, and she's still choosing him over me anyhow! Nobody cares if I live or die! I'm going to get high and hopefully die.

That day before my mother came home I left to find some crack. I had been out of the neighborhood for three years but as I said before if a person wants to find some drugs they can find the drugs. I found some crack and somewhere that I could get high too! It was just one catch though, if you smoked at someone else's house you had to either pay them or buy them drugs too. That wasn't a problem for me because I had money in my pocket. I was greeted at the door of the crack house as though I had never left. I had been away for 3 years but was greeted with hugs and kisses and was told to make myself comfortable. I had a funny feeling deep down in my belly, thinking to myself, "Why am I doing this'? The first hit was the best hit as I began to smoke the cocaine. I dropped a rock of the crack into the stem of the pipe carefully, skillfully making sure that it did not drop on the floor. I slowly put my lips on the mouthpiece of the pipe, lips swerved around the top of it to make sure none of the smoke would escape. Then I flicked the lighter, when the flame appeared I moved the lighter slowly toward the stem of the pipe with the eyes of a tiger making sure that the tip of the fire connected with the tip of the crack. Crack, Crack, Sizzle, Sizzle were the sounds of hell. As I began to inhale, the venomous vapors were entering my bloodstream, taking over every cell in my body, every part of my brain. I began to feel as if I was floating in thin air. Floating to a place where there weren't any worries, no sorrows, just me watching my life float away in a bowl of smoke. Woaaa that was nice! A few seconds passed before I passed the pipe and let someone else get a turn.

When it came back to me I took another long drag allowing myself to lose myself in the bowl of smoke. I did it, I'm back in hell.

The ritual went on for about 8 hours until my money ran out. After not smoking anything for about half of an hour reality began to set in. Then I remembered it was Sunday morning. I was supposed to go to church in the Bronx and see my boys. Reality was beginning to set in. High and frantic I went to the person that I had been spending my money with all night, the person who had all of my money in his pocket. I told him the situation about me having to go to church and he started to laugh hysterically at me. I asked him if I could borrow $10 dollars so that I can leave and go to the Bronx to see my boys. He laughed and told me to get out of his face before he slapped me. What am I going to do? What am

I doing here? I don't belong here! Then I remember someone talking about the power of prayer. I've never prayed before to get out of situations but, I have heard people say that prayer works. As I was thinking and looking around me everyone that was in the house started looking demonic. I saw odd contoured faces, oblong arms on some, and shapeless bodies and heard loud laughter and some screaming. I began to cry and pray, I've never done that before. "God please, please help me. Please get me out of here. Please God. If you do I will never ever use drugs again in my life. God please, I need a miracle please" crying to God with tears streaming down my eyes while the demonic figures were laughing at me. Afterward I sat in a corner while they were getting high and laughing at me. About 15 minutes passed with no human solution. All of the sudden, the person that had all of my money in his pocket came over to me, he handed me $20 dollars, he looked at me square in my eyes and said, "Take this money and go. I don't ever want to see your face again". Oh my God, thank you God, thank you! He answered my prayers!

I ran out of that crack house, walked to the subway, got on the train and went to the Bronx. I remember thinking to myself that God had saved me from the den of demons and I had to make it to church. When the train arrived in the Bronx I ran from the subway to the church thinking that I would be on time for the beginning of the service but God had another plan for me. As I got in front of the church everyone was coming out of the church, the service was over. NO, NO I missed service? I have to get inside. I must get inside! I pushed past the people who were coming out, ran into the church, fell face down on the altar, screaming out to God, "I can't do this anymore God! I need you! Help me please! I need you God. I can't stop using on my own"! I was crying, screaming, my nose was running, but I didn't care. I had nothing, I had no one and I used drugs again after being clean for 3 years. I had heard that if you cry out to God he will hear you and help you. After all God just did when I was in the crack house right? After all he just did it for me a couple of hours ago when I was in that pit full of demons. While I was crying on the altar of the church someone came near me, they put their hand on my shoulder, bent down with me and began praying for me. I felt something lift out of my soul and I knew right then that God was going to change my life and he did. He heard me.

Because I had smoked crack again after 3 years, everyone wanted me to go into another program but, I tried to assure them that God had delivered from my addiction and I wasn't ever going to touch another drug again. They didn't believe me. My family wanted me to go into another program called "New Life for Girls" which was a Christian facility. I refused to go there, I didn't care where they wanted me to go or what they wanted me to do because I knew deep down in my soul the drug life was over for me. So the Pastor of the church gave me another chance to live in the Girls House. I went back there, got another job, saved my money to move out and hopefully regain custody of my children. I began going back to church and staying drug free. I was blessed with some great jobs too. At one time I worked at the Commodities Exchange as a floor clerk working hand in hand with a broker that traded gold, silver and copper. After I left that job because I was tired of hearing bells all day long, I went to work for a marketing firm on 5th Avenue. That's when it all happened.

I was working at the Coolidge Company, a direct mail marketing firm on 5th Avenue in Manhattan. An hour before I can call it quits for the day I developed an excruciating headache. On the way home I stopped at the pharmacy to pick up some Tylenol. The headache was so severe, I thought I had a migraine headache so I bought a bottle of water and popped the aspirin before I got on the train home. My head hurt so bad, I was contemplating going to the hospital but, I didn't. When I got home, I didn't go straight to the daycare as I usually did to pick up my children, instead I laid down on my bed in the dark holding my head because it hurt so bad. After an hour or so, the headache went away. I was able to pick up my children and get a good night's sleep.

The next day I woke up feeling refreshed and ready for a new day. I am usually out of the bed by 6:00 am, I get the kids ready for daycare and school by 7am and then I would get on the train to go to work by 7:30 in the morning. Great! I don't have a headache today. At about 3:00 pm a meeting was called at the job to go over some last minute details for the company picnic in Central Park the next day. I was excited because we were going to play softball, I used to play softball and was very good at playing short center. There were other activities that were going to take place but whenever someone mentioned softball excitement ran through my bones. Besides, other direct mail marketing companies would be there and it would be a good chance to network. Food, family, fun and friends, a person couldn't ask for more. After work I went to Model's and bought a new pair of New Balances and a Yankee baseball cap. If I were going to be one of the team captains I had to look the part. After shopping at Model's I went to Virgils Barbecue Restaurant to buy some food to take home. I bought some ribs, chicken and baked beans so I didn't have to cook that night. When I got home my headache reared its ugly head again. So I picked up the kids, thank God they had already eaten so I just put the food in the refrigerator.

I opened my eyes the next morning so excited about the company picnic in Central Park today. I will be taking my son with me. He is 2 years old and I know he will have so much fun. It's been a while since I've played a game of softball. I guess it's like riding a bike, once you've learned to ride you never forget how. I was wishing that I would hit a home run and the ball would fly over the Ritz Hotel. It's time to get out of bed and start my day I told myself. As I sat up on my bed and swung my feet around to the floor I felt a tingling sensation throughout my entire body. I started to stand up but instead I fell on the floor and could not move. My daughter was sleeping in my bed and when I fell to the floor she called out to my oldest son who was sleeping in the living room to come and help. My son asked me what was going on, all I could say is, "Please. I don't know what's going on, call the ambulance now" in a very low voice. My eyes were open but, I could not move or feel anything. The ambulance came; they put me on a stretcher and took me into the vehicle, they were taking me to St. Barnabas Hospital in the Bronx. With all the commotion some of my neighbors came out of their houses, one of them took the kids. I overheard people talking and saying that I was having a stroke. As the ambulance arrived at the hospital, hospital staff was waiting at the door ready to take me in. I remember

looking into people's faces and hearing voices, but the

next time I would hear anyone's voice was after my

surgery later on in Columbia Presbyterian Hospital. At the

same time I was having a stroke, I was also bleeding on

the right side of my brain. At St. Barnabas Hospital I

became unconscious so they had to get me to Columbia

where they were equipped and specialized in

neurosurgery. I had what is called in medical terms a sub-

achranoid hemorrhage, a vessel in my brain burst on the

right side causing my brain to fill up with blood.

Remembering when I received a second chance at

life. Remembering the day I thought that my life was

over. Remembering the day I woke up to see my family

standing around me. Remembering the day I had tubes,

wires attached to my body, bandages covering my head

and staples connecting my flesh in hopes of fusing my head back together again. Remembering the beeps of the machines, the doctors and my family, the Priests and the Rabbi's praying over me. Remembering the day I had a brain aneurysm and a stroke.

Beep, beep beep, Beep, beep beep, Beep…Why can I hear everything but I see nothing. Everything around me is so dark. WOW! Is that the light that I've heard so much about? Do I follow it? Or do I remain still and just look at it, watch it? This place is dark and I can see a small light afar off? No. I think I will move towards the light. Wait! I can't move! I can hear people but…"Why can't I move" I asked the people. Why isn't anyone answering me? Don't they hear me? "Why can't I move" I ask again. Again there is no response. I say to myself, "They can't hear me" so I lay there immobile, silent, only hearing other voices and my own voice in my head. Although I wanted someone to hear me and was scared I did not cry, inside of my mind I was not crying in that dark place with the light shining. Many have said that when they were in a coma or thought they were dead afar off in their mind they saw a shining light. They said they saw the light and moved toward it and when they did they were once again in the land of the living. Well, I saw that shining light and a voice said to me, "It's not time yet, I have something for you to do".

My Aunt, who rarely comes out of her house because she has vertigo, came to the hospital to visit me. This is the same aunt who at one time took custody and cared for my sons and, she constantly prayed for me without ceasing for my deliverance from drug addiction. She came to the hospital to visit me a couple of weeks later. I could not see her but, I could hear her. She was

praying over me and then she asked me if I wanted

Lemon Coconut Cake or Chocolate Chip Cookies. If I

could've spoken at that moment I would have said," Lady

are you crazy! I can't speak and you're asking me what I

want to eat"? Only God knew that if I could speak I

would've said Lemon Coconut Cake. I loved that cake!

Then she asked me again but this time she said, "Do you

want Lemon Coconut Cake or Chocolate Chip Cookies?

Answer me?" With all of my strength, probably because I

wanted the cake so bad, I murmured in a low voice very

slowly, "caaaaak". She started jumping for joy, I could

hear her. She rushed out of the room to tell the doctors I

spoke and had awakened. Of course, when they got to

my room I was asleep again but, it was a different type of

sleep. Before I was sleeping in a coma and no one knew if

I were ever going to wake up but, this time I was sleeping just because I was tired.

I woke up from a deep deep sleep, thanking God I was in the land of the living once again. The doctors came into my room to finally remove the bandages off of my head which I thought was good sign that everything was going to be ok. When I was allowed to look into the mirror at myself which I haven't done it about a month the tears streamed down my face. The right side of my head was the size of a watermelon and the left side was a normal size. On the right side of my head all of my pretty long hair was cut off and the skin of my head was sewn together and connected by surgical staples. I looked like a monster. Did I think that I would ever be the same again? No! Never in a million years would I have ever thought that I would be the same again but no one knows that plans that God has for us. The doctors said that I would

need extensive therapy to regain my speech, mobility and

thought patterns. I would have to learn to read, write,

walk and talk all over again as if I were a little child.

I began to speak with a slow slur, unintelligible

words. I still could not walk, I couldn't even walk to the

bathroom and I had to be spoon fed. I began to go to

therapy every other day. Some days I would have speech

therapy, some days I would go to therapy so that

hopefully I would be able to walk again. I didn't know

what my name was, what day or year it was it was

horrible. It's very frustrating when someone asks you a

question that you are supposed to know the answer to

and you don't. I started to think that I would never be

able to think again, talk again or walk again but God had a

different plan for my life. Eventually, over time and

numerous hours of both types of therapy I began to get a little better. When it was time for me to be discharged from the hospital, I spoke with a slur and I walked with the assistance of a walker. I knew that God was going to heal me. Before I left though, the hospital staff gave me a party, they were calling me the "Miracle Child" because they said they've never seen anyone who went such an ordeal and has progressed the way that I did. They said that most people do not survive from a brain aneurysm and a stroke at the same time. It was a miracle that I survived. But if they knew like I knew, it was God who sustained me, it was him who seen me through it all. Why? Because God has something for me to do!

After being home for 3 months taking different medications and walking with the assistance of a walker, enough was enough! I spoke to my boss, the CEO of the marketing company, and asked him if there was any chance that I could come back and work for him. He asked me to come into his office so that we could talk. My speech wasn't totally back to normal, I still spoke with a slur but it wasn't as bad as before. I went to his office to speak to him, he agreed to allow me to come back to work on a trial basis. He told me not to worry about anything, not even my medical bill that it would all be taken care of. So I returned to work the next week. Being that my job was in direct marketing, I had to speak to clients on a daily basis to help them with their marketing strategies including the demographics in which they should send their mailings to. Although I spoke with a slur, I had to be honest with the clients so they didn't think I was drunk. If I was asked about my speech I would tell them that I just had major brain surgery but I was getting better. Also, I would thank them for their patience with me and they appreciated my honesty. God was truly working in my behalf. As time went on with a lot of repetition I became much better at speaking and walking although it wasn't totally back at 100 percent.

As my faith in God began to grow and, with a lot of hard work I started to get better. I wanted to go to ministry school because I felt that I needed to do more in the church. After all, God gave me a second chance at life and I owed him. I signed up to attend ministry school. It was a school specializing in evangelism especially street evangelism. Upon completion we would know how to effectively evangelize in the streets, conduct street meetings, and evangelize to people on a one to one basis and much more. The classes were very intense. We had to memorize Isaiah 53 in order to graduate amongst other things. I had always seen people speaking in tongues in the church but I never understood what it was. All I knew is that it was something that I wanted because it seemed as though it was a special language that connected you to God.

At the end of ministry school there was a graduation ceremony. During the ceremony there was a period of prayer for anyone who wanted to receive the baptism of the Holy Spirit. Of course I went forward. I'll never forget it as long as I live. I was being prayed for and I felt as though something was welling up deep inside of my belly and it needed to come out. I was told to speak, speak in the heavenly language that God had given to me. I was afraid but something, words wanted to escape from my mouth but I couldn't say anything, I wasn't about to let it go. Whatever was welling up inside of me became more and more intense, whereas I could no longer hold it inside of me, it had to come out. Something wanted to

burst from inside of me like a river, I wanted to scream,

shout and let it go. Finally, I couldn't hold on any longer

and I opened my mouth and began to speak in a language

that was unknown to me, I was speaking the heavenly

language that God had instilled inside of my belly. Some

of the other students, Pastors and people began to cry.

They praising God and blessing God for the miracle that

had just occurred. At first I did not understand what was

happening to me, but whatever happened I knew that it

was God who did it.

God was beginning to use me, isn't that what my

aunt said he was going to do? A couple of weeks later I

went to a service at church on a Sunday morning. The

Pastor was preaching a wonderful message on that

Sunday. While he was delivering the message to the

people, as he was preaching I began to feel the same sensation throughout my body as I felt the day I first spoke in tongues. I started to feel a heat throughout my body. After the preacher preached his message he called an altar call for people who needed prayer or wanted to accept Jesus Christ into their hearts but no one stood up. He said it a second time and again no one responded to the call. I heard a voice in side of my head say to me distinctly, "Go stand up to the altar and begin to pray for the people". "What! Surly not me! The Pastors of the church will be upset with me. They didn't tell me to do that. I will not move from my seat". Again I heard the voice of the Holy Ghost tell me to go up to the front of the church and begin to pray for the people. I was hesitant but, the Holy Ghost told me twice I knew I had to obey. As I looked around at my family, church members, and the clergy sitting in their seats quiet waiting for people who would be bold enough to go up to the altar, I stood up. I got up out of my seat, walked up to the front of the church, and stopped just below the pulpit where the Pastor was preaching from. The people were looking at each other because no one else was bold enough to go up to the front, they may have thought I was going up for prayer, but God had something else in mind. All eyes were on me as I stood there waiting for the Lord to tell me what to say. I turned around to face the people with a fire in my eyes and flowing throughout my body. I began to speak, I was not afraid any longer. I do not remember the words that I spoke but I do remember this, I was speaking the words that God was giving me to speak.

After I spoke briefly, I called another altar call with boldness and a sensation of fire throughout my soul, my spirit and my body. Looking out into the faces of the congregation I saw people crying, praising God and looking at me in awe. I thought that by now the Pastors in the church would have told me to sit down but nobody did. So I asked the question, "Does anyone need prayer or want to accept Jesus Christ as their Lord and Savior come up and let me pray for you? Make your way to the Alter and let me pray for you". To my surprise, people began to fill the aisle and come down to the altar. I motioned for the Pastors that were there to help me because I needed help there were a lot of people. I myself began to cry for the people who God directed me to lay my hands on and pray for them. God allowed me to touch the very souls of the people I was praying for and one by one they began to fall out on the floor praying and crying. What? The fire that was inside of me, the anointing that flowing through me, this never happened to me before! God what is going on? My God, my God!

Oh hallelujah! Thank you Jesus!! When I had finished

doing what God wanted me to do on that day, I walked

back to my seat staring directly ahead of me. I did not

turn my head to the left or turn my head to the right but I

looked straight ahead with my mind focused on Jesus,

focused on the glory of God, thanking him for using me

mightily for his glory. And that was just the beginning...

III

A couple of years had come and gone. Living in the big city began to get a bit burdensome and I became uncomfortable living there I wanted more I wanted better. But the big question was where do I go from here God? One of my sisters had moved upstate in New York with her family in a quaint little town in the Hudson Valley. Every time we'd go and visit my sister I'd joke around with them saying, "One day I'm going to live here and you see that Walmart over there, I'm going to work there too." Everyone would all laugh at me in the car but little did they know I actually saw myself in a vision working in that exact Walmart. Believe it or not within the next year I was working in that exact Walmart. You see I left the big city a couple of months prior to that, stayed with my sister until I could get established and my second job in this new town we were living in was Walmart.

The town we were living in was very different from where we had come from. In New York City the streets are always busy, the people are always busy and sometimes it seemed as though it was hard for me to stay focused. Moving upstate was one on the best things that happened to me. The air that I breathed was cleaner, the people were friendlier and it was not congested with cars, buses, trains and the hustle and bustle that you would see every day in the inner city. Frank Sinatra called New York the city that never sleeps but upstate in New York it seemed as though the people actually slept. Sleep, peace and rest is exactly what I needed.

The education system was different here too. Most of the inner city schools had very low budgets along with overcrowded classrooms. Many schools in the inner city did not have computers of textbooks for the students but not in this town, in this town the schools were beautiful and education was definitely a priority. The classrooms were spacious equipped with textbooks and computers, desks and chairs enough for everyone. My youngest son was about 6 years old at the time. It was his time to begin going to school. I had to register him to attend primary school so I took the day off of work so that my son and I can go to the school and get him started in the place where he would begin to learn. At the beginning of the orientation one of the teachers began to give their presentation concerning the curriculum for the new students. She was explaining that because of their age it was very important that to teach them skills that they would need to help them succeed in their future. She said that at this age a childs mind is equivalent to a sponge. They want to soak up any information any way they can and they are able to. So in saying that the children would be studying their basic reading, writing and math skills along with a little bit of World Geography, Science and Algebra. "Algebra!!" I thought to myself. I was in disbelief! I was absolutely shocked at the words that were coming out of her mouth! So I raised my hand to ask her to please repeat what she had just said. Raising my hand slowly I said, "Excuse me but I'm a little confused. Can you please repeat what you have just said?" The woman acknowledged me and said," Of course. The children will be learning their basic reading and writing skills along with mathematics. At the same time we will be planting seeds of World Geography, Sciences and Algebra". After she spoke those words again which was like music to my ears, my tears began to well up in my eyes. Thank you Jesus I kept saying over and over again in my mind. The Lord has led me to a place where my child will be able to get a decent education, a place where a good education is a priority to people.

After the orientation and registration I knew that I would stay in this town for a while.

Something was missing though. I was employed, I was living in a great apartment, the schools were great but there was still a void in my heart. I'd watch Christian television when I had the opportunity but I needed to find a church to attend. I miss going to church...I liked to watch Bishop TD Jakes, Bishop Neil C. Ellis and Joyce Meyers on TV they always had a message that would speak to my spirit. I would love to hear Joyce Meyers say, "If you can believe it, you can receive it" but nothing can beat physically being in the house of the Lord.

One Sunday my friend and I decided that were going to find a church to go to soon. We weren't sure where we were going to go but, we were sure we were going to find one. That very same day as we were sitting outside enjoying the fresh air and this woman walks up to us out of nowhere and asks us if we went to church. We told her that we believed in Jesus Christ but we did not have a home church. "Why don't you guys visit the church that I go to one day? I think that ya'll would like it there. The Pastor is a young man but he can sure preach and teach the bible. I think ya'll would have a good time" she said. My friend and I looked at each other and began to laugh hysterically. "Why are you laughing she asked us?" Then I told her that just before she approached us we were talking about going to church the next Sunday.

The following Sunday we went to church. We went to the church that the woman invited us to. During the service the congregation danced and sang worship songs. They sang songs that I was familiar with from the church that I used to attend in the Bronx. I was glad about that because I knew the words. That young Pastor preached on that Sunday morning that penetrated my soul. He preached the bible in a way that I understood and only saw on television. He preached a message of hope and salvation to the congregation like there was a fire on him that can only come from spending a lot of time with God. When the service was over I felt as if this is the church where I am supposed to be. This is the place where God wants me to be. In this church I could grow and learn more about the bible. So after visiting for a couple of weeks my friend and I decided to join the church. We decided to join this new family of believers.

A couple of weeks went by and I started to become comfortable around my new family, my church family. I began to sing on the worship team that was something I always wanted to do but I was afraid. I would sing in the shower or at home when no one else was there but to sing in front of people that was another story. Nonetheless I gave it a shot. Every person on the team had to sing a solo on alternating Sundays. During one of our rehearsals the team leader told me that it was my turn to lead a song. "Which song is the one I that you want me to lead" I asked. "Anointing fall on me" she told me. Ohhh nooooo! Not that song! I liked to sing with the others but to sing a song like that, by all by myself was overwhelming. "You can do it. Just close your eyes and sing unto the Lord" she said. Although I was frantic I agreed to lead the song because I wanted to be obedient to my leader. I practiced and I practiced and I practiced some more. I practiced until I thought I could sing the song without any problems whatsoever. Finally the day arrived when I was going to make my debut. I sang that song with everything I had inside of me. My voice was clear and beautiful. I was shocked, I've never sang so clear. And then I realized by singing this particular song I was actually asking the holy ghost to pour out is anointing on me. In the book of Matthew chapter 7 and verse 7 the bible says," Ask and it shall be given unto you, seek, and ye shall find, knock, and it shall be opened unto you." I asked and his anointing fell on me.

A couple pf weeks later an announcement was made in service that a new class was starting for people who were there 2 years or more if they were interested. The class would teach them how to write a sermon, spiritual warfare and church etiquette. I knew that I had only been attending the church for less than a year but nonetheless if I was allowed to sit in the back of the class I would be very grateful. I mustered up every bit of confidence I had inside of me and asked the instructor if she would allow me to sit in the back of the class. "I would be as quiet as a church mouse" I told her. "You would have to ask Pastor. I can't make that decision. If he says yes you are more that welcome to sit in the back of the class." She told me.

So I ran with it. As soon as she said that to me I ran upstairs to the Pastors office, knocked on the door awaiting my welcome. "Come in" a voice said from behind the door. I opened the door nervous and excited at the same time to see this young anointed man of God that's been preaching up a storm on the pulpit. "Excuse me Pastor but I hope I am not disturbing you, I have a quick question. There is a class that's beginning soon and I know I haven't been here for 2 years but may I please be allowed to sit in the back of the class while it is in session"? "Why would you want to do that?" he asked. "Because I want to know more about the Lord, because I want to learn more about the church and Jesus." I told him. I was scared of his reply, nervous and doubtful that I would be rejected. Who did I think I was anyhow, to sit amongst people who were more knowledgeable than I was in the things of God. They didn't know me and I didn't really know them but nonetheless I wanted to learn. When my Pastor said yes my tears began to stream from my eyes. At that moment I was overwhelmed and overjoyed that he said yes. Truly God is a miracle worker. I was told to let the instructor know that he agreed to me sitting in the class.

During the classes I remained as quiet as a church mouse listening to the students and the instructor as they spoke during the class or went over their assignment. Although at times I wanted to participate I kept quiet because that was the agreement. I was in absolute awe of the interpretation of the scriptures, the prayers and the fun that the class had during their time together. Almost a year went by and the classes were going to end soon. One of the requirements was that each student must prepare a trial sermon to present to the class. Wow! What an honor to preach the word of God! And then it happened. "You too" the teacher said looking in my direction. I was wondering who she was talking to so I turned around looking behind me to see if there was someone else there. "I want you to prepare a trial sermon to present to the class. You can choose any scripture you like and you have 15 minutes." Before I can say no I said YES. I almost went into shock! I was just supposed to be sitting in the back of the class minding my own business and now I had to prepare a message? Oh my God! What am I going to talk about? What am I going to preach about?

The day finally came when we must stand and present our trial sermons. I had given one before but that was in the Bronx when I went through ministry school specializing in street evangelism. The sermon I gave in the Bronx was on Matthew 6:25-34 but this time it had to be something else. So I chose John 3:16 which states,

"For God so loved the world that He gave His only begotten Son, that whoever believes in Him should not perish but have everlasting life". I asked God to give me strength to speak the words he wanted me to say, I prayed that the Lord would take away the nervousness I had in my belly to speak in public. Many are taught to look above the heads of your audience or to focus on one person so that you would not get nervous. All of that went out of the window when I began to preach the gospel. I spoke with authority, clarity and I looked at each person in the eyes as I went forth with my presentation. As I looked at the people I noticed that all of their eyes were fixated on me shaking their heads in awe and disbelief. I heard people saying, "Tell the truth!" or "You better preach" which made me feel as though I was on the right track in what I was saying to them. When I had finished, while I was walking back to my seat a couple of the students began clapping and I heard someone say, "I knew it! She's an Evangelist!" What!! I am a what! I'm an Evangelist! What the heck is an Evangelist? Well whatever an Evangelist is it sounded good so I said thank you and continued to go to my seat.

Two weeks after everyone gave their trial sermons there was going to be a graduation ceremony for the students who participated and completed the courses. They were told to wear black attire. Black skirts for the women and black slacks for the men along with white shirts or blouses. The ceremony was absolutely beautiful with everyone in uniform and unity. The students were called by name one by one to come up to the pulpit and receive their licenses to preach the gospel. I was so happy for them that I cried for each and every one of them. I thanked God because he allowed me to be a part this elite group of people that were being licensed to preach and teach the Gospel of Jesus Christ. I wanted to be licensed too but it was ok after all I was able to learn more and that was a blessing in itself. "Tyraine Campbell please come up." I heard a voice say as though I was dreaming. "Please come forward" I heard. I stood up as though I was inside of a dream. Confused and excited I walked up to the front of the church. "We are presenting you with this license to preach and teach the gospel of Jesus Christ in the state of New York. Now go forth and tell the world that Jesus is Lord! Godspeed Evangelist!" and then I was handed my license. What a mighty God we serve! Unbelievable! God is awesome! My destiny is beginning to unravel itself.

For the next couple of years my life consisted of work, raising my family on my own (with God's help) and church. I became the Overseer of the Outreach Ministry and I preached the word of God and evangelized to hurting souls in the streets.

Then one day it happened. The Holy Spirit spoke to me. The Holy Spirit spoke in my ear and said," There something that you have to do? "You must write a book. You must tell this story of how God has delivered you, saved you and set you free. Others need to know of the goodness, the grace and the mercy of "Him who is able to do exceedingly and abundantly above all that we ask or think, according to the power that works in us" (Ephesians 3:20). "Me write a book? I can't write a book! I wouldn't know where to begin or how to begin. Surely I'm not hearing right!" " You have to write a book" the spirit of God said to me again. "You will start at the beginning" I was instructed. "But God, I don't have the necessary skills to write a book." "Everything that you need I have equipped you with. Go back to school. Enroll in the College for the next semester. Go back to school.

There is where you will obtain the skills to write." I heard

the Holy Spirit say. Who was I to say no so I started to

inquire at the local college to find out what I had to do to

enroll for the next semester.

After many trials (which God bought me through) I was

able to enroll in college majoring in Human Services

because in studying Psychology and Sociology I can be

more effective in ministry having an idea of how the mind

works and how this society governs itself. But there were

so many days and nights while I was in school that I

wanted to quit, I wanted to throw in the towel but God

said no. So many times I wanted to pull my hair out, I

wanted to scream to the top of my lungs but God said no.

How many people know that if God bought you to it He

will bring you through it! There were times that I thought

I had failed a course during one of the semesters only to

find out that I had passed it. During the midst of it all God was moving me forward giving me the strength that I needed to pursue what He had told me to do because there He had a bigger plan for me. God had other plans for me other than being confined within the four wall of the church. So I continued going to school and I joined the Christian Club on the campus.

And then it was time…

I've been in school for two and a half years and it was almost time to graduate from college. I have learned to be disciplined and write research papers as long as 20 pages, I have studied the psyche as well as many societal issues. I have learned and studied advance Algebra as I had to take 3 Algebra courses and passed each one. Also I have learned and studied a plethora of History courses including Ancient Rome, Greece, Africa, Middle East and their customs and religions. I have gained a vast amount of knowledge that at one time I did not think would ever be possible for me. As I was walking home from school one day it happened again...

Now it is time...

I heard a voice clear as day telling me," Now it's time to tell your story". "How am I going to tell my story?" I asked. "I don't people to know about all the stuff I did, see how horrific my life has been. I am a new person, you said so yourself. I am a new creation in Christ, all things are passed away and I'm someone new." I said. "That's the reason you need to tell your story. There are so many people who are struggling, so many souls that are dying because they haven't any hope. Because you have endured many trials, hardships and tribulations and I have allowed you to live through it all you must tell your story. Because the people need to know that I love them with an unconditional love, an everlasting love and I can save them. You need to tell your story because there is no one that is beyond the reach of God, I want you to let them know that regardless of anything and everything they have been through in their lives that God is a mighty God and can save them if they want to be saved. You must let them know that I can do abundantly exceedingly all that they could ever think or imagine. You must let them know that there is a God and He is as real as the air that we breathe".

So I began to write…

It was not an easy task. Many times I would lay in my bed in a fetal position crying and asking God why? Why me? Why did I have to go through so much pain? No one I knew suffered as much as I did but as I wrote of some of my experiences is when I received my healing. Healing from the hurt, the pain that had kept me bound and bitter for many years. I began to forgive not only my step father but people that I have forgotten about, people that I put into a compartment in my brain that I left there for many years. There were times I wanted to give up but I knew that this book was part of my destiny so I prayed and I pushed until I received a breakthrough. I didn't write anything for a couple of months, I had what one may call writers block and I couldn't understand why. One night as I was praying it dawned on me that I did not finish my assignment. I knew that giving up was not an option but actually in my mind it was. Who would care about a story of a person like me? Who did I think I was anyhow writing a book, no one would read it anyhow! There are two options in this life. Either you can give up, quit, throw in the towel or you can keep pressing, keep going and persevere. One night I was going to make my choice. I was leaning toward the first option which is quitting. I cried so hard, I cried out to God asking him why? Why can't I finish my assignment? Why can't I write anymore? Why? Why? Why? I felt so alone. Surely after this story any friends that I do have will not want to have anything to do with me, people will treat me as though I have the plague. They will laugh at me, talk badly about me. I feel as though I am already alone and now I could only imagine what it would be like whenever this book is published. Forget it! I'm done! No more! I can't do this anymore! Then the sweet still voice spoke into my ear again and said," My child you are not alone, for I am with you until the end of days. I am the Alpha and the Omega, I am the beginning and the end. I I have blessed you and I have favored you. Go forth, the windows of heaven are opening up for you. Do not worry about what others say or even do have I not already delivered you from the snare and the pit. It is I that have blessed you and favored you not man. Have no fear for I am with you until the end of days and I will make your name great saith the Lord." After I heard those words I leaped out of my bed laughing, dancing and worshipping God. I grabbed my laptop and began to write again. The words were flowing freely off of my fingers and on to my computer. And then I realized, the revelation fell on me like a ton of bricks, I had to be free of others opinions about me.

I had to be free to trust God and God alone! I was so worried about what other people thought about me that I was getting ready to flush my assignment down the toilet. No one wants to be alone that's a given but when you come to the realization God loves you for you whoever you may be that's all you need. He is our provider, He is our protector and He has our best interest at heart. Although it may not seem like you can make it you can. Just hold on and keep the faith because the race is not

given to the swift or the strong but to those who endures
to the end.

Now I am finished, I am free and this is my purpose. My
purpose is to spread the gospel to all those who would
hear. To let people know that God is real. He saved me,
He delivered me and He has set me free and He can do
the same for you if you only believe. The Bible says in the
book of John chapter 3 verse 16 that," For God so loved
the world that He gave His only begotten Son, that
whosoever believes in Him should not perish but have
everlasting life." I challenge everyone who reads my book
to choose life, chose it today because tomorrow is not
promised to us. Although some of us may not see the
bigger plan for our lives believe me when I tell you there
is one. Just hold on, don't give up, and don't throw in the
towel Gods got a plan for you. Praying for all who read
this book may the Lord keep you and bless you. May he

make his light shine upon you and give you peace! A

peace that surpasses all understanding knowing that GOD

IS and He is a rewarder of those who diligently seek him.